JENNIFER CHIAVERINI

The Loyal Union Sampler
from
ELM CREEK QUILTS

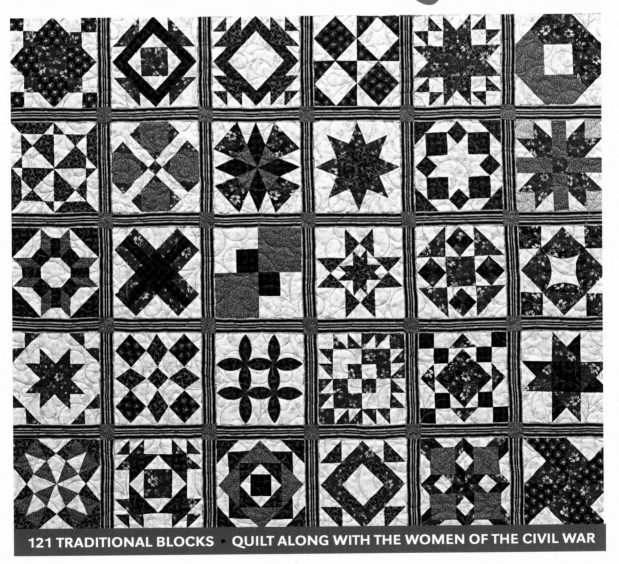

121 TRADITIONAL BLOCKS · QUILT ALONG WITH THE WOMEN OF THE CIVIL WAR

C&T PUBLISHING

Text copyright © 2013 by Jennifer Chiaverini

Photography and Artwork copyright © 2013
by C&T Publishing, Inc.

Publisher: Amy Marson

Creative Director: Gailen Runge

Art Director: Kristy Zacharias

Editor: Deb Rowden

Technical Editors: Alison M. Schmidt, Teresa Stroin,
Carolyn Aune, and Mary Flynn

Cover Designer: April Mostek

Book Designer: Kristen Yenche

Production Coordinator: Jessica Jenkins

Production Editor: Alice Mace Nakanishi

Illustrators: Tim Manibusan and Aliza Shalit

Photo Assistant: Mary Peyton Peppo

Photography by Christina Carty-Francis and Diane Pedersen
of C&T Publishing, Inc., unless otherwise noted

Published by C&T Publishing, Inc., P.O. Box 1456, Lafayette, CA 94549

Library of Congress Cataloging-in-Publication Data

Chiaverini, Jennifer.

The Loyal Union Sampler from Elm Creek Quilts : 121 Traditional Blocks - quilt along with the women of the Civil War / Jennifer Chiaverini.

pages cm

ISBN 978-1-60705-765-9 (soft cover)

1. Patchwork--Patterns. 2. Quilting--Patterns. 3. Patchwork quilts. I. Title.

TT835.C454 2013

746.46--dc23

2013002785

Printed in China

10 9 8 7 6 5 4 3 2 1

DEDICATION

To Elm Creek Quilts fans everywhere whose admiration
for *The Union Quilters* inspired this book.

ACKNOWLEDGMENTS

I am grateful to the wonderful quilting friends who contributed blocks
to several of the Loyal Union Sampler quilts featured in this book:

Barbara Ahlf • Tanya Anderson • Annette Ashbach • Donna S. Austin • Fernande Authuys • Pamela Craft Avara
Yvonne Bagnell • Jenet Hiller Bakke • Cynthia Barger • Chiquita Barnes • Beverley Fredericka Barnett
Kathleen N. Bart • Colleen Bartell • Roxanne Baumann • Diane Becka • Marianna Bergkamp • Judith Berry
Connie Boulay • Dorothy Bourdo • Debra Braaksma • Josie Bricco • Alice Brooks • Marie Z. Brown
Rita Broyles • Pamela Bruner • Debra Bourdo Bryant • Jorja Burke • Dawn Burks • Jeanne M. Butler
Julia Callanan • Bethaney Campbell • Phyllis K. Campbell • Maria Catalano • Grace Chandler • Debbie Childress
Patty Clayton • Michelle Clubine • Karen Jackson Coté • Jane Cotter • Mary A. Crowther • Laurie Cwerenz
Karen Cyson • Shannon Davin • Kathy Decker • Carolyn Dell • RoseMarie DeNatale • Lynda Goldstein DeTray
Linda L. Diaz • Barb Dinger • Jacqueline Dorsey • Louise Dutove • Laurie Edvardsson • Donna Eisman
Janet Ann Elia • DeAnna Elliott • Esther Else • Sharon Everson • Elise Fare • Julie Faulkner • Jean Fischer
Cecile Flegg • Patricia H. Frey • Lou Jane Gatford • Barbara Geiseman • Maggy Giorgetti • Julie Goedeke
Sharon Goodno • Bonnie L. Gottsacker • Mary Grafton-Krogh • Carrie Graziano • Joelle Gregorcich
Donna Mae Grim • Joyce Munz Hach • Rebecca Hafemeister • Karen Hallman • Katherine Hallman
Ruthann Haluschak • Patricia J. Harrell • Joanne Harris • Kate Thompson Hayes • Jennifer Heeres
Kathryn Heusinkveld • Heather Hickling • Donna Hoerig • Melanie Bassett Hudson • Karen Huffman
Gay L. Jackson • Barbara Jennekens • Connie Jeske • Nancy Joiner • Mary Jordan • Paula R. Jungerberg
Cheryl A. Karl • Robin Kessell • Barb Killen • C. Louise King • Sheri Klaich • Susie Klostermann
Lynette Konitzer • Sharon Kopp • Elni Langeveld • Valerie Langue • Rhonda S. Lauer • Cathy Leitner
Kathe Lemmerman • Jan Lennstrom • Carole A. Lienau • Linda Long • Cheryl Lorden • Jennifer Lorenzo
Judy Losinski • Wanda Lowrey • Deb Luebke • Debbie Madigan • Donna Malchow • Joanne Maner
Leonore V. Mangold • Debbie Markowitz • Kathy McAdam • Pauline McBride • Judy McCabe Krudwig
Sandra McLay • Jane Miller • Terry Miller • Ann L. Milne • Patricia J. Minorik • Barbara Miska • Susan Mokler
Lis Moore • Faith Morlan • Maryanna Moseby • Jan Mullarkey • Nancy Munson • Carol Netzler • Karen S. Nuss
Gerry Olson • Carolyn Oltman • Kathy Oppelt • Beth Owen • Nancy Panozzo • Karen Pantony • Susy Parrott
Terri L. Pearce • Penny S. Pember • Sharon Petersen • Sharon Phillips • Cherie Pingle • Cheryl Plourde
Suzanne Prather • Becky Preston • Gloria Prillwitz • Karen Pruehs-Kozlowski • Ginny Radloff • Patricia Rahrig
Katell Renon-France • Shirley Van Vlierden Robbins • Anne Ida Røkeness • Kay D. Romahn • Marcia J. Rowe
Rita L. Sainz • Kris Scharfenberg • Jennifer L. Schmidt • Susan P. Schultz • Sue-Z Schwab • Christina Seaman
Ellie Marie Senne • Robin Shaw • Joanie Sheridan • Deb Sherrock • Darlene Slater • Bernadette Smelik
Debbie Saddler Snook • Sandy Söderblom • Julie Gilman Spokane • Linda Starkey • Chris Stein • Jane M. Stevens
Shelley Stevens • Melba Stockdale • Rosemary Strube • Anita Marie Rose Stumpf • Catherine R. Taylor • Cindy Temple
Connie Tessier • Sue Thorland • Fran Threewit • Barb Tibbals • Marie Tovo • Lisa A. Treptow • Joan Tyree
Annelies van den Bergh • Mirjam van der Meulen • Caroline Van Maele-Delbrouck • Carol VanTreeck
Lynn Vegafria • Sue Wagenaar • Agnes M. Waksmunski • Kay M. Walker • Lorianne Walker • Susan Wehmeyer
Fran Weintraub • Kathy Welliver • Patricia Wendt • Liesbeth Wessels • Sharon Wetherall • Cindy Wilson
Kristine Winkler • Linda Witt • Krista Yokum • Marsha Zackschewski • Katie Zenk • Kim Zenk • Carin Zwaneveld

I offer special thanks to Anne Ida Røkeness and Annelies van den Bergh, who made their own exquisite
Loyal Union Samplers for the Gallery, and to Sue Vollbrecht, who beautifully quilted most of the quilts within these pages.
I also thank my mother, Geraldine Neidenbach, for binding many of the quilts for me.

This book would not have been possible without the contributions of the wonderful creative team at C&T Publishing,
especially Gailen Runge, Deb Rowden, Alison M. Schmidt, Teresa Stroin, Carolyn Aune, Mary E. Flynn, April Mostek,
Kristen Yenche, Jessica Jenkins, Alice Mace Nakanishi, Tim Manibusan, and Aliza Shalit. Many thanks to you all.

Contents

HOW TO FIND EACH BLOCK IN THE QUILT

We've given you an easy way to find any block within the quilt. The blocks are all coded with a letter for the row and a number for the column that the block is in (see diagram on page 99). For example, Rhode Island (page 75) is coded as Block I-4. If you go down to Row I and over to Column 4, you will find the Rhode Island block. If you want to create a quilt exactly like this, place your blocks according to their grid numbers.

The Union Quilters and the Loyal Union Sampler

> "I am not accustomed to the use of language of eulogy; I have never studied the art of paying compliments to women; but I must say, that if all that has been said by orators and poets since the creation of the world in praise of women were applied to the women of America, it would not do them justice for their conduct during this war."
>
> —*President Abraham Lincoln, Washington, D.C., March 8, 1864*

I've always been fascinated by history, especially women's roles in American history, and writing the Elm Creek Quilts novels has provided me with a wonderful opportunity to research many different regions, quilting styles, and historical eras. My longtime readers—especially fans of *The Runaway Quilt*, *The Sugar Camp Quilt*, *The Lost Quilter*, *The Union Quilters*, and *Mrs. Lincoln's Dressmaker*—will not be surprised to learn that if I had to choose a favorite historical period to write about, I would choose the antebellum and Civil War eras.

The Civil War era was a tumultuous and transformative time for the United States, showing the best and worst of humanity in stark contrast. Looking back, we discover great moral failings alongside true heroism in the struggle for justice, equality, and freedom. My personal heroes are people who face adversity with moral courage and dignity, whose hunger for justice and compassion for others lead them to stand up for what is right, even at great risk to themselves. In my writing, my favorite characters usually possess similar qualities—although sometimes, at a crucial moment, they may fail to do what is right and must endure the consequences. What slavery and the Underground Railroad say about our country—that we are capable of both great moral failings and tremendous goodness—resonates strongly even today, perhaps especially today. As a creative person, I am drawn to explore and try to understand that conflict.

Several characters in *The Union Quilters* first appeared in earlier Elm Creek Quilts novels set during the antebellum period. As I reflected upon their past adventures and conflicts, I thought it would be interesting to explore how they responded to the Civil War when it finally erupted. My characters' experiences are based on historical accounts of real woman on the home front and real soldiers at war.

As *The Union Quilters* opens, it is 1862, and the men of Water's Ford, Pennsylvania, rally to answer Mr. Lincoln's call to arms, spurring the women of the Elm Creek Valley into their own battle to preserve the nation.

Dorothea Granger, dismayed by her scholarly husband's bleak descriptions of food shortages and illness in the soldiers' camps, marshals her friends to "wield their needles for the Union" and provide for the men's needs. Her friend Constance Wright staunchly supports her husband as he is repeatedly turned away from serving in the Union army because of the color of his skin, and she is determined to help him secure both the privileges and the responsibilities of citizenship. Anneke Bergstrom's pacifist husband does not enlist, but his safety becomes her shame—one that compels her to work ceaselessly for the Union cause to prove her family's loyalty. A gifted writer committed to hastening the war's end, Gerda Bergstrom takes on local Southern sympathizers in the

AULANI HO'OILO, 62″ × 80″, designed and assembled by Jennifer Chiaverini, pieced by Jennifer Chiaverini and friends, machine quilted by Sue Vollbrecht, 2012. The "Elm Creek Quilts: The Aloha Quilt Collection" fabrics used in this quilt were provided by Red Rooster Fabrics.

SANTA ROSA SUNSET, 49″ × 49″, designed by Jennifer Chiaverini, pieced by Jennifer Chiaverini and friends, quilted by Sue Vollbrecht, 2012. The "Elm Creek Quilts: Rosa's Collection" fabrics used in this quilt were provided by Red Rooster Fabrics.

pages of the *Water's Ford Register*, risking the wrath of the Copperhead press.

While the women work, hope, and pray at home, the men they love confront loneliness, boredom, and harrowing danger on the bloody battlefields of Virginia, Maryland, and Pennsylvania. Anxious for news, the women share precious letters around the quilting circle, drawing strength and comfort from one another as they witness from afar the suffering and deprivation their husbands, brothers, sons, and sweethearts must endure. It falls to the Union Quilters to provide for the soldiers at the front and the wounded veterans who have come home, to run farms and businesses, and to protect their homes and families when the Confederate army threatens the Elm Creek Valley. Their new independence will forever alter the patchwork of town life in ways that transcend even the ultimate sacrifices of war.

In *The Union Quilters*, as in history, Union and Confederate women alike made quilts for soldiers to use in camps and in hospitals. They sewed and raffled off quilts to raise funds to support important causes, and they quilted to express themselves artistically during a time of national strife and personal turmoil. On the Northern home front, the demands of war thrust women into new roles, for they suddenly needed to support and provide for the men who had always been cast in the role of their protectors. This was an unsettling transition, and yet, for many women, it offered an exhilarating sense of independence. The women's advocacy for their husbands, sons, and brothers empowered them. The volunteer organizations they created to provide food, clothing, medicine, and other essential goods for the soldiers allowed them to step beyond the private, domestic sphere and participate in a new, public realm outside of the traditional political structure from which they were excluded. Accounts of women's volunteer organizations, especially the Ladies' Aid Association of Weldon in Pennsylvania, inspired the activities of the Union Quilters in my novel. Like their fictional counterparts, the Ladies' Aid Association of Weldon constructed a hall to host fundraisers and incorporated and maintained ownership of an important cultural center and civic resource, despite strong male opposition. Control of the hall provided the women with significant influence and power in their town, leverage they had not previously possessed.

In the novel, to raise money to build a hall of their own, Anneke, Dorothea, and the other Union Quilters embark upon an ambitious plan to create the Loyal Union Sampler. They invite every woman in the Elm Creek Valley to contribute a 6″ patchwork block of her own design or a favorite traditional pattern that was not particularly well known. They also ask each participant to provide templates and suggestions for how best to construct her chosen block. Once completed, the blocks would be sewn together into an exquisite sampler, quilted by the finest needleworkers in the valley, and then offered up in a raffle. The fortunate winner would claim the quilt, templates, and instructions, thus winning a lovely quilt as well as an extraordinary catalog of quilt patterns—enough to keep even the most industrious quilter pleasurably occupied for years to come. In the end, the Union Quilters' plan is a tremendous success—before long, the quilt is completed, and construction on Union Hall, the site of many future fundraisers for the troops and veterans, has begun.

I'm sure it's no secret that I enjoy making the quilts featured in my novels, as my previous five pattern books from C&T Publishing will attest. I made the first Loyal Union Sampler on my own, using fabrics from "Elm Creek Quilts: Anneke's Collection" from Red Rooster Fabrics. To make the other lovely samplers featured in this book, I followed the Union Quilters' example and enlisted the help of 212 talented quilters and Elm Creek Quilts fans from around the world. Many of my helpers were members of the *Sylvia's Bridal Sampler* mailing list, while others signed up at the 2010 Wisconsin Quilt Expo. Supplied with block patterns and fabrics from various Elm Creek Quilts collections, my volunteers set themselves to the task. Before long, I had collected the hundreds of lovely blocks that fill the pages of this book. I assembled the blocks into several different tops, which were beautifully quilted by Sue Vollbrecht. Annelies van den Bergh of the Netherlands and Anne Ida Røkeness of Norway—two longtime quilting friends whose quilts were featured in *Sylvia's Bridal Sampler from Elm Creek Quilts*—went above and beyond by making entire Loyal Union Samplers all their own. I'm sure you'll agree that all of these volunteers are not only generous but also marvelously talented!

If the story of my volunteers, the Union Quilters, and the real, historical women who inspired my characters has captured your imagination, I hope you'll enjoy making your own Loyal Union Sampler. Keep in mind that these 121 new 6″ × 6″ (finished) blocks are the same size as those in *Sylvia's Bridal Sampler*, so you can swap favorite blocks between the two quilts to create a wonderful new sampler all your own. However you use these patterns, I hope you'll find your endeavor both rewarding and fun and that you'll proudly display your Loyal Union Sampler, both finished and as a work-in-progress, to inspire your own circle of quilters.

As quilters across the country and around the world, united we stand!

Loyal Union Sampler

⊞ THE QUILT ⊞

Finished quilt: 98″ × 98″ | **Finished block: 6″ × 6″** | **Number of blocks: 121**

LOYAL UNION SAMPLER
Machine pieced and appliquéd by Jennifer Chiaverini, machine quilted by Sue Vollbrecht, 2012. The "Elm Creek Quilts: Anneke's Collection" fabrics used in this quilt were provided by Red Rooster Fabrics.

For detailed information on piecing and construction techniques, please refer to Start Quilting with Alex Anderson *(from C&T Publishing),* The Art of Classic Quiltmaking *by Harriet Hargrave and Sharyn Craig (from C&T Publishing), or any basic quiltmaking book.*

Fabric Requirements

Note: *These figures are approximations only, based on fabric with 42" usable width. Yardage amounts will vary based on your fabric choices for each individual block.*

Light beige: 7 yards

Reds: 3½ yards

Medium blues: 3 yards

Dark blue: ¾ yard

Green: 3 yards

Very light brown: ¾ yard

Light brown: 5⅝ yards (for blocks, cornerstones, and inner border) or less if inner border is cut on crosswise grain, instead of lengthwise as shown in quilt

Medium brown: ½ yard

Dark brown: 1½ yards

Assorted light multicolored florals: ¼ yard or 1 fat quarter each

Small stripe: 1½ yards (for sashing)

Wide floral stripe: 3¾ yards (for outer border and binding)

Batting: 106" × 106"

Backing: 9 yards

ABEL'S FAVORITE — BLOCK A-1

1. From light beige fabric, cut 1 square 3½″ × 3½″ (A), cut 1 square 4¼″ × 4¼″ (C), and cut 2 squares 2⅜″ × 2⅜″ (D).

2. From medium blue fabric, cut 4 squares 2″ × 2″ (B) and 6 squares 2⅜″ × 2⅜″ (D).

3. Quick-Pieced Half-Square Triangle (HST) Units: Make 4 quick-pieced HST units.

a. Draw a diagonal line from corner to corner on the wrong side of a light beige D square.

b. Pair a light beige D square with a medium blue D square, right sides facing. Sew ¼″ on both sides of the drawn line.

c. Cut on the solid line to make 2 HST units. Press toward the medium blue fabric.

d. Repeat Steps a–c with the remaining light beige and medium blue D squares to make a total of 4 HST units.

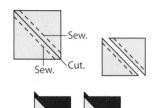

4. Quick-Pieced Flying Geese Units: Make 4 quick-pieced Flying Geese units.

a. Draw a diagonal line from corner to corner on the wrong side of 4 blue D squares.

b. Place 2 medium blue D squares on top of the light beige C square, right sides facing, corners overlapping, and drawn lines aligned.

c. Sew a scant ¼″ on both sides of the drawn lines. Cut apart on the drawn lines. Press toward the darker fabric.

d. Place a medium blue D square on one of the units created in Step c, right sides facing, with the drawn line at a right angle to the previous seam. Sew a scant ¼″ on both sides of the drawn line. Cut on the drawn line. Press toward the light beige fabric to make 2 Flying Geese units.

e. Repeat Step d with the remaining unit created in Step c and the remaining medium blue D square to make 2 more Flying Geese units.

5. Quick-Pieced Square-On-Point Unit: Make a quick-pieced square-on-point unit.

a. Draw a diagonal line from corner to corner on the wrong side of the medium blue B squares.

b. Matching one corner and aligning adjacent sides, place a medium blue B square on the light beige A square, right sides facing.

c. Sew on the drawn line.

d. Trim fabric ¼″ away from the sewn line. Press the seam toward the medium blue fabric.

e. Repeat Steps b–d with a second medium blue B square in the opposite corner.

f. Repeat Steps b–d with 2 additional medium blue B squares in the remaining corners.

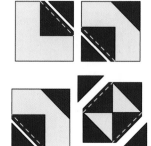

6. Arrange the block segments into 3 rows as shown in the block assembly diagram. Sew the segments together into rows. Press. Sew the 3 rows together. Press.

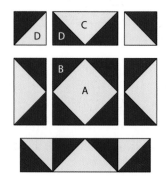

ABIGAIL'S SWING

The template patterns are on page 105.

1. Use template A to make 8 triangles from light beige fabric and 8 triangles from red fabric.

2. Use template B to make 1 square from light brown fabric.

3. From light brown fabric, cut 2 squares 3⅛″ × 3⅛″. Cut each square in half diagonally once to make 4 C triangles.

4. Sew 1 light beige A triangle to each long side of 1 red A triangle. Repeat to make 4.

5. Sew 2 of the units created in Step 4 to opposite sides of the light brown B square from Step 2.

6. Sew 2 red A triangles to opposite sides of the remaining units created in Step 4.

7. Use Y-seam construction to sew the units created in Step 6 to opposite sides of the B square unit created in Step 5, sewing seams in the order and direction indicated in the diagram. Do not sew into seam allowances.

8. Sew the light brown C squares to the corners of the block.

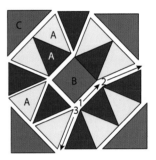

A HOUSE DIVIDED

1. From a light multicolored floral fabric, cut 1 square 5¼″ × 5¼″. Cut the square in half diagonally twice to make 4 multicolored floral triangles (A). Set 2 aside to use in another project.

2. From medium blue fabric, cut 4 strips 1¼″ × 6″. Sew a strip to the left short leg of each A triangle, matching the end of the strip to the right angle but extending the strip

¼″ beyond the base before trimming the excess fabric. Press. Sew a blue strip to the other short leg of the triangle, again extending the strip ¼″ beyond the base before trimming the excess fabric. Press. Carefully trim the excess fabric to make 2 right triangles with a base of 7¼″.

3. From a second light multi-colored floral fabric, cut 1 square 7¼″ × 7¼″. Cut the square in half diagonally twice to make 4 multi-colored floral B triangles. You will need only 2; save the others for another project.

4. Sew 1 B triangle to each of the A triangle units created in Step 2. Press toward the B triangle.

5. Sew the units created in Step 4 together in pairs. Press. Trim the block to 1 square 6½″ × 6½″ for a 6″ × 6″ finished block.

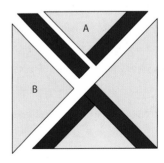

ANNEKE'S CHOICE

The foundation patterns are on page 105.

1. Make 4 of foundation paper piecing pattern A using red, light beige, and dark brown fabrics. Press.

2. Make 4 of foundation paper piecing pattern B using red, light beige, and dark brown fabrics. Press.

3. Make 1 of foundation paper piecing pattern C using red and dark brown fabrics. Press.

4. Sew 2 foundation paper piecing A units to opposite sides of a foundation paper piecing B unit to make the top row. Press. Repeat to make the bottom row.

5. Sew 2 foundation paper piecing B units to opposite sides of the foundation paper piecing C unit to make the center row. Press.

6. Sew the 3 rows together. Press.

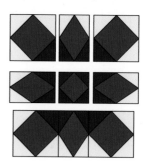

ANTIETAM

The template patterns are on page 106.

1. From light beige fabric:

■ Make 4 squares using template A. *Note:* Save this template. You will be using it for other blocks too.

■ Cut 4 squares 1⅞″ × 1⅞″. Cut each square in half diagonally once to make 8 triangles (B).

2. From medium blue fabric:

■ Make 4 pentagons using template C.

■ Cut 2 squares 3¼″ × 3¼″. Cut each square in half diagonally twice to make 8 triangles (D).

3. From red fabric:

■ Make 1 square using template A.

■ Cut 4 squares 1½″ × 1½″ (E).

4. Sew 2 medium blue D triangles to adjacent sides of 1 light beige A square. Press. Repeat to make 4.

5. Sew 1 light beige B triangle to 1 red E square. Press toward the red fabric. Repeat to make 4.

6. Sew 1 light beige B triangle to 1 medium blue C pentagon. Press toward the medium blue fabric. Repeat to make 4.

7. Sew a unit created in Step 5 to a unit created in Step 6. Press. Repeat to make 4.

8. Sew 2 units created in Step 7 to opposite sides of the red A square. Press.

9. Sew 2 units created in Step 4 to opposite sides of a unit created in Step 7. Press. Repeat to make another.

10. Arrange the block segments into 3 diagonal rows as shown in the block assembly diagram. Sew the rows together. Press.

The template patterns are on pages 105 and 106.

1. From medium blue fabric, make 5 squares using template A.

2. From green fabric:

- Make 8 triangles using template B.

- Cut 2 squares 1⅞″ × 1⅞″. Cut each square in half diagonally once to make 4 triangles (E).

3. From light beige fabric:

- Make 8 triangles using template C.

- Cut 2 squares 3¼″ × 3¼″. Cut each square in half diagonally twice to make 8 triangles (D).

4. Sew each B triangle to a C triangle. Press toward the green fabric. Sew the B/C triangle units together into 4 pairs. Press.

5. Sew 1 green E triangle to the end of each B/C unit. Press.

6. Sew 2 units created in Step 5 to opposite sides of a medium blue A square. Press.

7. Sew 2 light beige D triangles to the adjacent sides of each remaining medium blue A square. Press.

8. Sew 2 units created in Step 7 to opposite sides of a unit created in Step 5. Press. Repeat to make another identical unit.

9. Arrange the block segments into 3 diagonal rows as shown in the block assembly diagram. Sew the rows together. Press.

The template patterns are on page 106.

1. From light beige fabric:

- Cut 4 squares 2″ × 2″ (A).

- Cut 2 squares 2¾″ × 2¾″. Cut each square in half diagonally twice to make 8 triangles (B).

- Make 4 rectangles using template D.

2. From red fabric:

- Make 4 squares using template C.

- Cut 1 square 2⅝″ × 2⅝″ (E).

3. From dark blue fabric, cut 2 squares 2¾″ × 2¾″. Cut each square in half diagonally twice to make 8 triangles (B).

4. Sew 2 dark blue B triangles to adjacent sides of each light beige A square. Press. Sew a light beige B triangle to each dark blue B triangle. Press. Repeat to make 4 block corners.

5. Sew 2 light beige D rectangles to opposite sides of the red E square. Press toward the red fabric.

6. Sew 2 red C squares to opposite ends of a light beige D rectangle. Press toward the red fabric.

7. Sew the units created in Steps 5 and 6 together to make the central uneven Nine-Patch. Press.

8. Sew 2 block corners from Step 4 to opposite sides of the uneven Nine-Patch. Press. Attach the other 2 block corners. Press.

1. From light beige fabric, cut 4 rectangles 1¼″ × 3⅛″ (B), 4 squares 1⅜″ × 1⅜″ (C), 8 squares 1¾″ × 1¾″ (D), and 1 strip 1⅜″ × 12″.

2. From green fabric, cut 1 square 1¼″ × 1¼″ (A) and 1 strip 1⅜″ × 12″.

3. From red fabric, cut 8 squares 1¾″ × 1¾″ (D).

4. Sew the green strip to the light beige strip. Press toward the green fabric. Use a rotary cutter to cross-cut 8 strips 1⅜″ wide. Abutting seams and aligning different colors, sew the strips together to make 4 Four-Patches.

5. Refer to Quick-Pieced HST Units (page 14, Abel's Favorite, Step 3) to make 16 quick-pieced HST units with the 8 red and 8 light beige D squares.

6. Sew the HST units together to make 4 pairs and 4 mirror-image pairs. Press.

7. Sew a paired HST unit to each Four-Patch as shown. Press.

8. Sew a light beige C square to each mirror-image triangle-square pair as shown. Press.

9. Sew a unit created in Step 7 to a unit created in Step 8. Press. Repeat to make 4.

10. Sew 2 units created in Step 9 to opposite sides of a light beige B rectangle to make the top row. Press. Repeat to make the bottom row.

11. Sew the remaining light beige B rectangles to opposite sides of the green A square. Press.

12. Sew the 3 rows together. Press.

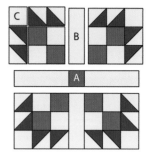

BLOCKADE

The template pattern is on page 106.

1. From light beige fabric, make 4 trapezoids using template A.

2. From light brown fabric:

- Cut 1 square 4¼" × 4¼". Cut the square in half diagonally twice to make 4 triangles (B).

- Cut 1 square 2⅜" × 2⅜". Cut the square in half diagonally once to make 2 triangles (C).

3. From medium blue fabric:

- Cut 1 square 4¼" × 4¼". Cut the square in half diagonally twice to make 4 triangles (B).

- Cut 1 square 2⅜" × 2⅜". Cut the square in half diagonally once to make 2 triangles (C).

4. Sew each C triangle to a light beige A trapezoid. Press.

5. Sew each light brown B triangle to a medium blue B triangle, taking care to place the colors as shown. Press.

6. Sew each B/B triangle pair to a unit created in Step 4, taking care to orient the B/B pair correctly. Press.

7. Sew the block quarters into 2 rows as shown in the block assembly diagram. Press. Sew the rows together. Press.

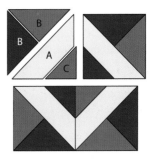

BROKEN PATH

1. From light beige fabric:

- Cut 2 squares 4¼" × 4¼". Cut each square in half diagonally twice to make 8 A triangles. *Note:* You will need only 6. Set aside 2 for use in another project.

- Cut 1 rectangle 1½" × 3½" (B).

2. From green fabric:

- Cut 2 squares 4¼" × 4¼". Cut each square in half diagonally twice to make 8 A triangles. *Note:* You will need only 6. Set aside 2 for use in another project.

- Cut 2 rectangles 1½" × 3½" (B).

3. Sew the 2 green rectangles to opposite sides of the light beige rectangle. Press.

4. Sew 2 light beige A triangles to the green rectangles. Press.

5. Sew 2 green A triangles to the remaining sides of the central unit. Press.

6. Sew a green A triangle to a light beige A triangle along the short sides. Press. Repeat to make an identical unit. Make 2 mirror-image units.

7. Following the block assembly diagram for correct color placement, sew 2 green/light beige triangle units to opposite sides of the block center. Press.

8. Attach the mirror-image green/light beige triangle units. Press.

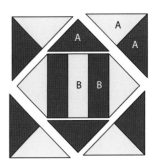

1. From light beige fabric, cut 16 squares 1⅞″ × 1⅞″ (A) and 1 square 2½″ × 2½″ (C).

2. From medium blue fabric, cut 8 squares 1⅞″ × 1⅞″ (A).

3. From red fabric, cut 2 squares 3¼″ × 3¼″ (B).

4. Refer to Quick-Pieced Flying Geese Units (page 14, Abel's Favorite, Step 4) to make 8 quick-pieced Flying Geese units with the 2 red B squares and 8 light beige A squares.

5. Sew the Flying Geese units into pairs.

6. Refer to Quick-Pieced HST Units (page 14, Abel's Favorite, Step 3) to make 16 quick-pieced medium blue and light beige HST units.

7. Sew the HST units together to make 4 pairs and 4 mirror-image pairs. Press.

8. Sew matching units created in Step 7 into pairs. Press.

9. Sew 2 Flying Geese pairs to opposite sides of the light beige C square to make the center row. Press.

10. Sew an HST unit and a mirror-image HST unit to opposite sides of a Flying Geese pair to make the top row. Press. Repeat to make the bottom row.

11. Sew the 3 rows together. Press.

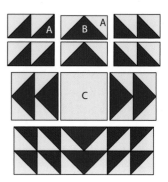

The template pattern is on page 106.

1. Use template A to make 4 squares from light brown fabric and 1 square from dark blue fabric.

2. From light beige fabric, cut 4 squares 2½″ × 2½″. From a corner of each square, trim a right triangle with legs 1⅛″ long to make 4 B pentagons. Draw sewing lines ¼″ in from the edges if desired.

3. From dark blue fabric, cut 4 rectangles 2½″ × 2⅝″. Cut 2 equal right triangles from the midpoint of a 2½″ side of each rectangle to make 4 C pentagons. Draw sewing lines ¼″ in from the edges if desired.

4. Sew 2 light brown A squares to opposite sides of the dark blue A square. Sewing only from point to point and not into the seam allowance, attach 2 light beige B pentagons to opposite sides of the row. Press toward the dark blue square.

5. Sewing only from point to point and not into the seam allowance, attach 2 dark blue C pentagons to opposite sides of a light brown A square. Use Y-seam construction to attach a light beige B pentagon to the unit. Repeat to make a second identical unit. Press toward the dark blue pieces.

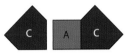

6. Use Y-seam construction to attach the units created in Step 5 to opposite sides of the unit created in Step 4, sewing in the order and direction indicated in the diagram. Press.

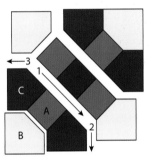

1. From light beige fabric, cut 4 squares 2⅜″ × 2⅜″ (A) and 1 square 3½″ × 3½″ (C).

2. From medium blue fabric, cut 1 square 4¼″ × 4¼″ (B).

3. From green fabric, cut 4 squares 2″ × 2″ (D).

4. Refer to Quick-Pieced Flying Geese Units (page 14, Abel's Favorite, Step 4) to make 4 quick-pieced Flying Geese units with the medium blue B square and 4 light beige A squares.

5. Sew 2 Flying Geese units to opposite sides of the light beige C square to make the center row. Press.

6. Sew 2 green D squares to opposite sides of each remaining Flying Geese unit to make the top and bottom rows. Press.

7. Sew the rows together. Press.

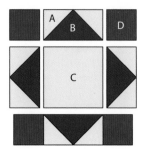

1. From light beige fabric:

- Cut 2 squares 2⅜″ × 2⅜″. Cut each square in half once diagonally to make 4 triangles (A).

- Cut 4 rectangles 1¼″ × 3½″ (B), 1 rectangle 2″ × 6″ (D), and 2 squares 2⅜″ × 2⅜″ (E).

2. From red fabric, cut 1 square 2⅝″ × 2⅝″ (C).

3. From medium blue fabric, cut 2 rectangles 1¼″ × 6″ (F) and 2 squares 2⅜″ × 2⅜″ (E).

4. Sew 2 light beige A triangles to opposite sides of the red C square. Press. Sew the remaining 2 light beige A triangles to the other sides. Press.

5. Refer to Quick-Pieced HST Units (page 14, Abel's Favorite, Step 3) to make 4 quick-pieced medium blue and light beige HST units with the E squares.

6. Sew the 2 medium blue F rectangles to opposite sides of the light beige D rectangle along the long edges. Press toward the medium blue fabric. Use a rotary cutter to crosscut 4 strips 1¼″ wide.

7. Sew each F/D/F strip to a light beige B rectangle. Press.

8. Sew 2 HST units to opposite ends of a unit created in Step 7 to make the top row. Press. Repeat to make the bottom row.

9. Sew 2 units created in Step 7 to opposite sides of the unit created in Step 4 to make the center row. Press.

10. Sew the 3 rows together. Press.

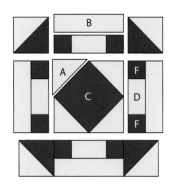

CASTLE WALL

The template patterns are on pages 106 and 107.

1. From light beige fabric, make 4 triangles using template E.

2. From very light brown fabric, make 1 octagon using template A and 8 rhombuses using template C.

3. From red fabric, make 8 trapezoids using template D.

4. From dark brown fabric, make 8 squares using template B.

5. Sewing from point to point only, sew 4 dark brown B squares to 4 opposite sides of the A octagon.

6. Sewing from point to point only, sew 2 C rhombuses to opposite sides of a brown B square. Use Y-seam construction to set a red D trapezoid into the angle. Press. Repeat to make 4 units.

7. Use Y-seam construction to set the units created in Step 6 into the 4 opposite angles created in Step 5. Press.

8. Use Y-seam construction to sew 4 red D trapezoids to the remaining sides of the brown B squares and C rhombuses. Press.

9. Sew the 4 light beige E triangles to the corners of the block. Press.

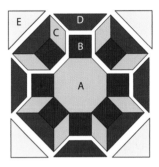

CHAMBERSBURG

The foundation patterns are on page 107.

1. Make 4 of foundation paper piecing pattern A using light beige and red fabrics. Press.

2. Make 4 of foundation paper piecing pattern B using light beige, red, and green fabrics. Press.

3. Make 1 of foundation paper piecing pattern C using light beige and green fabrics. Press.

4. Sew 2 foundation paper piecing A units to opposite sides of a foundation paper piecing B unit to make the top row; note the orientation of the green triangles. Press. Repeat to make the bottom row.

5. Sew 2 foundation paper piecing B units to opposite sides of the foundation paper piecing C unit to make the center row, referring to the block assembly diagram to orient the green triangles correctly. Press.

6. Sew the 3 rows together. Press.

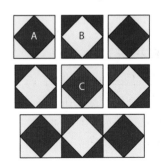

The template patterns are on pages 107 and 108.

1. From light beige fabric:

- Cut 2 squares 2¾″ × 2¾″. Cut each square in half diagonally twice to make 8 triangles (A).

- Make 4 triangles using template B. Flip the template and make 4 B reverse.

2. From light brown fabric, make 4 polygons using template C. Flip the template and make 4 C reverse.

3. From red fabric:

- Make 4 kites using template D.

- Cut 4 squares 1¼″ × 1¼″ (E) and 1 square 2⅝″ × 2⅝″ (F).

4. From medium blue fabric:

- Make 4 pentagons using template H.

- Cut 4 squares 1⅝″ × 1⅝″. Cut each square in half diagonally once to make 8 triangles (G).

5. Sew 1 light beige B and 1 light beige B reverse to each red kite to make the block corners. Press.

6. Sew 2 medium blue G triangles to adjacent sides of each red E square. Press. Sew 2 of these units to opposite sides of the red F square. Press. Sew the remaining 2 units to the other 2 sides to complete the block center. Press.

7. Sewing only from point to point and not into the seam allowance, sew 1 light brown C and 1 light brown C reverse to opposite sides of each medium blue H pentagon. Use Y-seam construction to set a light beige A triangle into each C/H angle. Press.

8. Sew 2 units created in Step 7 to opposite sides of the block center to make the center row. Press.

9. Sew 2 block corners to opposite sides of a unit created in Step 7 to make the top row. Press. Repeat to make the bottom row.

10. Sew the rows together. Press.

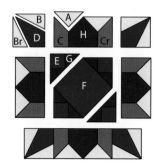

The template pattern is on page 108.

1. From light beige fabric:

- Cut 1 square 2½″ × 2½″ (B).

- Cut 8 squares 1½″ × 1½″ (C).

- Cut 2 squares 3¼″ × 3¼″. Cut each square diagonally twice to make 8 large triangles (A).

- Cut 2 squares 2¼″ × 2¼″. Cut each square diagonally twice to make 8 small triangles (E).

2. From red fabric:

- Cut 1 square 3¼″ × 3¼″. Cut the square twice diagonally to make 4 triangles (A).

- Make 4 squares using template D.

3. From medium blue fabric, cut 8 squares 1⅞″ × 1⅞″. Cut each square diagonally once to make 16 triangles (F).

4. Sew 2 small light beige E triangles to adjacent sides of a red D square. Press. Sew 2 medium blue F triangles to each unit. Press. Repeat to make 4.

5. Sew 2 units created in Step 4 to opposite sides of the light beige B square. Press.

6. Sew 2 light beige C squares to opposite ends of each of the remaining 2 units created in Step 4 to make 2 rows. Press.

7. Sew the 2 rows created in Step 6 to opposite sides of the unit created in Step 5 to create the central star. Press.

8. Sew 2 light beige A triangles to a red A triangle along the short sides. Press. Sew 2 medium blue F triangles to opposite ends. Press. Repeat to make 4.

9. Sew 2 units created in Step 8 to opposite sides of the central star to make the middle row. Press.

10. Sew 2 light beige C squares to opposite ends of each remaining unit created in Step 8 to make the top and bottom rows. Press.

11. Sew the 3 rows together. Press.

1. From light beige fabric:

- Cut 2 squares 1⅞″ × 1⅞″ (A).

- Cut 2 squares 2⅞″ × 2⅞″. Cut each square in half diagonally once to make 4 triangles (B).

- Cut 1 square 3¼″ × 3¼″. Cut each square in half diagonally twice to make 4 triangles (C).

2. From medium blue fabric, cut 4 squares 1⅞″ × 1⅞″. Cut each square in half diagonally once to make 8 triangles (D).

3. From light brown fabric:

- Cut 1 square 3¼″ × 3¼″. Cut each square in half diagonally twice to make 4 triangles (C).

- Cut 1 square 2½″ × 2½″ (E).

4. From dark brown fabric:

- Cut 2 squares 2⅞″ × 2⅞″. Cut each square in half diagonally once to make 4 triangles (B).

- Cut 2 squares 1⅞″ × 1⅞″ (A).

5. Refer to Quick-Pieced HST Units (page 14, Abel's Favorite, Step 3) to make 4 quick-pieced dark brown and light beige HST units with the A squares.

6. Sew 2 medium blue D triangles to each HST unit along the light beige edges. Press. Sew a light beige B triangle to each unit. Press.

7. Following the block assembly diagram for correct color placement, sew each light beige C triangle to a light brown C triangle. Press. Sew a dark brown B triangle to each pair. Press.

8. Arrange the block segments into 3 rows and sew. Press. Sew the 3 rows together. Press.

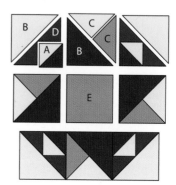

The foundation pattern is on page 108.

1. From red fabric, cut 1 square 2½″ × 2½″ (B).

2. From light beige fabric, cut 2 squares 3¼″ × 3¼″ (C).

3. From green fabric, cut 2 squares 3¼″ × 3¼″ (C).

4. Using light beige and red fabrics, make 4 of foundation paper piecing pattern A. Press.

5. Quick-Pieced Quarter-Square Triangle (QST) Units: Refer to Quick-Pieced HST Units (page 14, Abel's Favorite, Step 3a–c) and then follow the steps below to make 4 quick-pieced QST units with the light beige and green C squares.

a. On the wrong side of 1 HST unit, draw a diagonal line from a green corner to a light beige corner.

b. Place 2 HST units together, with right sides facing and green triangles facing light beige triangles. Align edges, abut opposing seams, and pin. Sew ¼″ on both sides of the drawn line.

c. Cut on the drawn line to yield 2 QST units. Press. Repeat with the remaining HST units to make 2 more QST units.

6. Sew 2 foundation paper piecing A units to opposite sides of a QST unit to make the top row. Press. Repeat to make the bottom row.

7. Sew 2 QST units to opposite sides of the red C square to make the center row. Press.

8. Arrange the block segments into 3 rows and sew. Press. Sew the 3 rows together. Press.

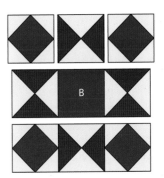

The foundation pattern is on page 108.

1. Using light beige and medium blue fabrics, make 2 of foundation paper piecing pattern A. Press.

2. Sew the 2 rows together. Press.

CONSTANCE'S PRIDE

BLOCK B-11

1. From light beige fabric, cut 2 squares 3¼″ × 3¼″. Cut each square in half diagonally twice to make 8 triangles (A).

2. From dark brown fabric, cut 4 rectangles 1¼″ × 3¼″ (B).

3. From light brown fabric:

- Cut 4 squares 1¼″ × 1¼″ (D) and 1 square 3¼″ × 3¼″ (E).

- Cut 4 rectangles 1⅞″ × 2¾″. Cut 2 equal 45° triangles from the midpoint of one narrow end to make 4 pentagons (C).

4. Sew 2 light beige A triangles to opposite sides of each light brown C pentagon to make the block corners. Press.

5. Sew 2 dark brown B rectangles to opposite sides of the light brown E square. Press.

6. Sew 2 light brown D squares to opposite sides of the 2 remaining dark brown B rectangles. Press.

7. Sew the 2 strips created in Step 6 to opposite sides of the unit created in Step 5 to make the central uneven Nine-Patch. Press.

8. Sew 2 block corners to opposite sides of the central uneven Nine-Patch. Press. Sew on the other 2 block corners. Press.

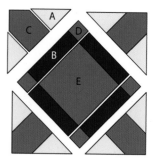

CORNERSTONE

1. Make 1 of the foundation paper piecing unit using light beige, medium blue, and red fabrics.

2. Trim to 6½″ × 6½″ (unfinished size) and press.

The foundation pattern is on page 109.

COTTON BOLL

1. Cut 4 squares 3½″ × 3½″ from light beige fabric.

2. From red fabric, cut 4 squares 2″ × 2″. Draw a diagonal line from corner to corner on the back of each square.

3. From dark brown fabric, cut 4 squares 2″ × 2″. Draw a diagonal line from corner to corner on the back of each square.

4. Matching one corner and aligning adjacent sides, place a red square on a light beige square. Sew on the drawn line. Trim fabric at the corner ¼″ away from the sewn line. Press the seam toward the darker fabric. Repeat with a second red square in the opposite corner. Repeat to make a second identical unit.

5. Repeat Step 4 using the 2 remaining light beige squares and the 4 dark brown squares.

6. Arrange the block quarters into 2 rows and sew. Press. Sew the rows together. Press.

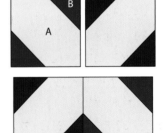

1. From light beige fabric:

- Cut 5 squares 2⅜″ × 2⅜″ (A). Cut 2 A squares in half diagonally once to make 4 triangles (C).

- Cut 4 squares 2″ × 2″ (B).

2. From green fabric:

- Cut 3 squares 2⅜″ × 2⅜″ (A).

- Cut 1 square 3⅞″ × 3⅞″. Cut the square in half diagonally once to make 2 triangles (D).

3. Refer to Quick-Pieced HST Units (page 14, Abel's Favorite, Step 3) to make 6 quick-pieced HST units with the green and remaining light beige A squares.

4. Sew 2 light beige C triangles to the green half of an HST unit. Press. Repeat to make 2.

5. Sew a green D triangle to each of the units created in Step 4. Press.

6. Sew a light beige B square to a dark edge of an HST unit as shown. Press toward the darker fabric. Repeat to make a total of 4 identical units.

7. Abutting seams and aligning solid light squares with HST units, sew the units created in Step 6 into pairs. Press.

8. Following the block assembly diagram, sew the block segments into 2 rows. Press. Sew the rows together. Press.

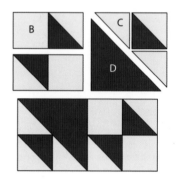

The template patterns are on pages 108 and 109.

1. From light beige fabric:

- Cut 1 square 3″ × 3″ (A).

- Make 8 squares using template B.

- Make 8 triangles using template C.

2. From red fabric, make 16 rhombuses using template D.

3. From dark blue fabric, make 4 trapezoids using template E.

4. Sew 2 dark blue E trapezoids to opposite sides of the light beige A square. Press. Sew the remaining 2 dark blue E trapezoids to the other 2 sides of the light beige A square. Press.

5. Sew 2 light beige B squares to opposite sides of the unit created in Step 4. *Note:* Sew from point to point only and not into the seam allowances. Sew 2 more light beige B squares to the other 2 sides. Press.

6. Sewing from point to point only, sew the red D rhombuses together in pairs. Press. Make 8.

7. Use Y-seam construction to sew a light beige C triangle to each red D rhombus pair. Press. Make 8.

8. Sewing from point to point only, sew a light beige B square to

a D/D/C unit along the right-hand side. Press. Repeat to make 4.

9. Sewing from point to point only and following the order and direction indicated in the diagram, sew a D/D/C unit to each D/D/C/B unit. Press. Repeat to make 4 block corners.

10. Use Y-seam construction to sew 2 block corners to opposite sides of the unit created in Step 7. Press. Sew the remaining 2 block corners to the other 2 opposite sides. Press.

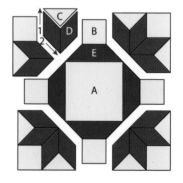

The template patterns are on pages 109 and 110.

1. From light beige fabric:

■ Cut 2 squares 1⅝″ × 1⅝″. Cut each square in half diagonally once to make 4 triangles (A).

■ Cut 3 squares 2¾″ × 2¾″. Cut each square in half diagonally twice to make 12 triangles (B).

■ Make 5 squares using template C.

2. From light brown fabric, make 8 squares using template C.

3. From medium blue fabric, make 4 rectangles using template D.

4. Sew 2 medium blue D rectangles to opposite sides of a light beige C square. Sew 2 light beige A triangles to opposite ends to make the center row. Press.

5. Alternating colors, sew together 2 light beige C squares and 3 light brown C squares. Sew a light beige B triangle to each end. Press. Repeat to make a second identical row.

6. Sew 2 light beige B triangles to opposite sides of a medium blue D rectangle. Press. Repeat to make a second identical row.

7. Sew 2 light beige B triangles to opposite sides of a light brown C square. Press. Sew a light beige A triangle to an adjacent side. Press. Repeat to make a second identical row.

8. Following the block assembly diagram, sew the 5 rows together, pressing after each addition.

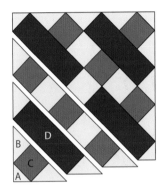

1. From red fabric, cut 2 squares 3½″ × 3½″ (A).

2. From dark brown fabric, cut 2 strips 1½″ × 8″ and 1 strip 1½″ × 4″.

3. From light beige fabric:

- Cut 8 squares 1½″ × 1½″ (B). Draw a diagonal line from corner to corner on the back of each square.

- Cut 1 strip 1½″ × 8″ and 2 strips 1½″ × 4″.

4. Matching one corner and aligning adjacent sides, place a light beige B square on a red A square. Sew on the drawn line. Trim fabric ¼″ away from the sewn line. Press the seam toward the dark fabric.

5. Repeat Step 4 with a second light beige square in the opposite corner, and then with 2 additional light beige B squares in the remaining corners.

6. Repeat Steps 4 and 5 to make a second, identical unit.

7. Sew the 2 dark brown 8″ strips to opposite sides of the light beige 8″ strip. Press toward the dark brown fabric. Use a rotary cutter to crosscut 4 strips 1½″ wide.

8. Sew the 2 light beige 4″ strips to opposite sides of the dark brown 4″ strip. Press toward the dark brown fabric. Use a rotary cutter to crosscut 2 strips 1½″ wide.

9. Sew 2 strips cut in Step 7 to opposite sides of a strip cut in Step 8 to make a Nine-Patch. Press. Repeat to make a second, identical Nine-Patch.

10. Arrange the block segments into 2 rows and sew. Press. Sew the rows together. Press.

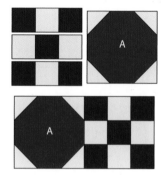

DEMOCRATIC WATCHMAN

1. From light beige fabric, cut 4 squares 2″ × 2″ (A) and 4 squares 2⅜″ × 2⅜″ (C).

2. From light brown fabric, cut 1 square 4¼″ × 4¼″ (D).

3. From green fabric, cut 1 square 3½″ × 3½″ (B) and 4 squares 2″ × 2″ (E).

4. Refer to Quick-Pieced Square-On-Point Unit (page 14, Abel's Favorite, Step 5) to make a quick-pieced square-on-point unit with the light beige A squares and the green B square.

5. Refer to Quick-Pieced Flying Geese Units (page 14, Abel's Favorite, Step 4) to make 4 quick-pieced Flying Geese units with the light beige C squares and the light brown D square.

6. Sew 2 Flying Geese units to opposite sides of the square-on-point unit to make the center row. Press.

7. Sew 2 green E squares to opposite sides of each remaining Flying Geese unit to make the top and bottom rows. Press.

8. Sew the rows together. Press.

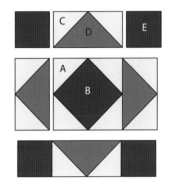

DIAMOND STAR

1. From light beige fabric, cut 4 squares 2″ × 2″ (A), 1 square 4¼″ × 4¼″ (B), and 2 squares 2⅜″ × 2⅜″ (C).

2. From medium blue fabric, cut 6 squares 2⅜″ × 2⅜″ (C).

3. Refer to Quick-Pieced HST Units (page 14, Abel's Favorite, Step 3) to make 4 quick-pieced HST units with 2 light beige and 2 medium blue C squares.

4. Refer to Quick-Pieced Flying Geese Units (page 14, Abel's Favorite, Step 4) to make 4 quick-pieced Flying Geese units with the 4 remaining medium blue C squares and 1 light beige B square.

5. Sew 2 light beige A squares to opposite sides of a Flying Geese unit to make the top row. Press. Repeat to make the bottom row.

6. Sew 2 HST units together following the block assembly diagram for placement. Press toward the medium blue fabric. Repeat to make a second, identical unit. Sew the 2 units together to make the central Pinwheel. Press.

7. Sew 2 Flying Geese units to opposite sides of the central Pinwheel to make the center row. Press.

8. Sew the 3 rows together. Press.

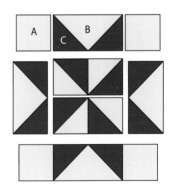

DOUBLE FOUR-PATCH

1. From light beige fabric, cut 2 squares 3½″ × 3½″.

2. From medium blue fabric, cut 1 strip 2″ × 8″.

3. From dark brown fabric, cut 1 strip 2″ × 8″.

4. Sew the dark brown strip to the medium blue strip. Press toward the darker fabric.

5. Use a rotary cutter to cut 4 strips 2″ wide from the strip set.

6. Abutting seams and placing dark brown squares facing medium blue, sew 2 strips together to make a Four-Patch. Press. Repeat to make a second Four-Patch.

7. Following the block assembly diagram for correct color alignment, sew a light beige square to each Four-Patch to make a row. Press.

8. Sew the 2 rows together. Press.

DOUBLE Z

1. From light beige fabric:

■ Cut 2 squares 2⅜″ × 2⅜″ (A).

■ Cut 1 square 4¼″ × 4¼″. Cut the square in half diagonally twice to make 4 triangles (B). (You will use only 2. Save the others for another block.)

■ Cut 1 square 4¼″ × 4¼″ (C).

2. From red fabric:

■ Cut 1 square 4¼″ × 4¼″. Cut the square in half diagonally twice to make 4 triangles (B). (You will use only 2. Save the others for another block.)

■ Cut 6 squares 2⅜″ × 2⅜″ (A).

3. Sew a light beige B triangle to a red B triangle. Press. Repeat to make a second, identical unit. Sew the 2 units together, abutting the seams and alternating colors, to make the central quarter-square triangle unit. Press.

4. Refer to Quick-Pieced Flying Geese Units (page 14, Abel's Favorite, Step 4) to make 4 quick-pieced Flying Geese units with 4 red A squares and 1 light beige C square.

5. Refer to Quick-Pieced HST Units (page 14, Abel's Favorite, Step 3) to make 4 quick-pieced red and light beige HST units with the remaining A squares.

6. Arrange the block segments into 3 rows as shown in the block assembly diagram. Sew the segments together. Press. Sew the 3 rows together. Press.

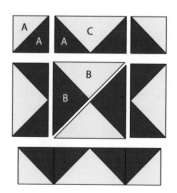

The template pattern is on page 110.

1. From light beige fabric:

- Cut 1 square 2¼″ × 2¼″. Cut the square in half diagonally twice to make 4 triangles (A).

- Cut 1 square 3¾″ × 3¾″. Cut the square in half diagonally twice to make 4 triangles (B).

- Cut 2 squares 3⅜″ × 3⅜″. Cut each square in half diagonally once to make 4 triangles (C).

2. From medium blue fabric, cut 1 square 3″ × 3″ (D).

3. From green fabric, make 4 rectangles using template E.

4. Sew 2 light beige B triangles to opposite sides of the medium blue D square. Press. Sew 2 more light beige B triangles to the other 2 sides. Press.

5. Sew 1 light beige C triangle to one side of each green E rectangle. Press.

6. Sew 2 of the units created in Step 5 to opposite sides of the unit created in Step 4. Press.

7. Sew 2 light beige A triangles to opposite ends of the remaining units created in Step 5. Press.

8. Sew the units created in Step 7 to the block. Press.

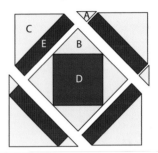

The foundation pattern is on page 110.

1. From light beige fabric, cut 1 square 4½″ × 4½″. Cut the square in half diagonally twice to make 4 triangles.

2. From red fabric, cut 2 squares 3⅞″ × 3⅞″. Cut each square in half diagonally once to make 4 triangles.

3. From dark brown fabric, cut 1 square 3½″ × 3½″.

4. Complete the foundation paper piecing pattern using the colors indicated. Press.

Traditional Piecing

1. From light beige fabric:

- Cut 4 squares 2″ × 2″ (A).

- Cut 2 squares 2⅜″ × 2⅜″. Cut each square in half diagonally once to make 4 triangles (B).

- Cut 1 square 4¼″ × 4¼″. Cut the square in half diagonally twice to make 4 triangles (C).

2. From light brown fabric:

- Cut 2 squares 2¾″ × 2¾″. Cut each square in half diagonally twice to make 8 triangles (D).

- Cut 1 square 2″ × 2″ (A).

3. From medium blue fabric, cut 3 squares 2¾″ × 2¾″. Cut each square in half diagonally twice to make 12 triangles (D).

4. Sew 2 medium blue D triangles to opposite sides of the light brown A square. Press. Sew 2 more medium blue D triangles to the remaining 2 sides. Press.

5. Sew 2 light brown D triangles to each light beige B triangle to make 4 Flying Geese units. Press.

6. Sew 2 medium blue D triangles to adjacent sides of each light beige A square. Press.

7. Sew each unit created in Step 6 to a Flying Geese unit created in Step 5, following the orientation in the block assembly diagram. Press.

8. Sew 2 units created in Step 7 to opposite sides of the unit created in Step 4 to make the center row. Press.

9. Sew 2 light beige C triangles to opposite sides of a unit created in Step 7 to make the top row. Press. Repeat to make the bottom row.

10. Sew the 3 rows together. Press.

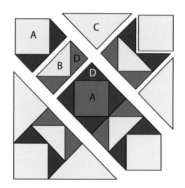

Foundation Paper Piecing

The foundation patterns are on page 111.

1. Make 1 of foundation paper piecing pattern A using light brown and medium blue fabrics. Press.

2. Make 2 of foundation paper piecing pattern B using light beige, medium blue, and light brown fabrics. Press.

3. Make 2 of foundation paper piecing pattern C using light beige, medium blue, and light brown fabrics. Press.

4. Sew the 2 foundation paper piecing B units to opposite sides of the foundation paper piecing A unit to make the center row. Press.

5. Sew the 2 foundation paper piecing C units to opposite sides of the center row. Press.

The template patterns are on page 111.

1. From red fabric, make 8 rhombuses using template A.

2. From light beige fabric:

- Cut 2 squares 3″ × 3″. Cut each square in half diagonally twice to make 8 triangles (B).

- Cut 2 squares 2½″ × 2½″. Cut each square in half diagonally twice to make 8 triangles (D).

- Cut 4 squares 1⅜″ × 1⅜″ (E).

- Cut 4 squares 1¾″ × 1¾″. Cut each square in half diagonally once to make 8 triangles (F).

3. From medium blue fabric, cut 1 square 3″ × 3″. Cut the square in half diagonally twice to make 4 triangles (B).

4. Using template C, make 8 rhombuses from medium blue fabric and 8 from dark brown fabric.

5. Sewing from point to point only and not into the seam allowances, sew the red A rhombuses together in pairs. Press.

6. Use Y-seam construction to sew a light beige B triangle to each red A rhombus pair. Press. Make 4.

7. Sewing from point to point only, sew a light beige B triangle to the right-hand side of each unit created in Step 6. Press.

8. Sewing from point to point only and in the order and direction indicated in the diagram, sew the units created in Step 7 into pairs. Press. Sew the pairs together. Press.

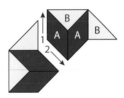

9. Sew 2 medium blue B triangles to opposite sides of the unit created in Step 8. Press. Sew 2 medium blue B triangles to the other 2 opposite sides to make the block center. Press.

10. Sewing from point to point only, sew a medium blue C rhombus to a dark brown C rhombus. Press. Repeat to make 4 pairs. Repeat again to make 4 mirror-image pairs.

11. Use Y-seam construction to sew a light beige D triangle to each pair created in Step 10. Press.

12. Sewing only from point to point, attach a light beige E square to 4 identical C/C/D pairs in the order and direction indicated. Press. Sew each of these units to a mirror-image C/C/D pair. Press.

Sew 2 light beige F triangles to opposite sides of each unit. Press. Repeat to make 4 block corners.

13. Sew 2 block corners to opposite sides of the block center. Press. Sew the remaining block corners to the other sides. Press.

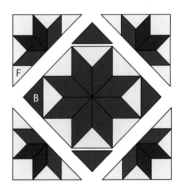

FARM IN THE VALLEY BLOCK D-4

1. From light beige fabric:

- Cut 1 square 3¼″ × 3¼″. Cut the square in half twice diagonally to make 4 triangles (A).

- Cut 2 squares 2⅞″ × 2⅞″. Cut each square in half diagonally once to make 4 triangles (B).

2. From green fabric, cut 2 squares 3¼″ × 3¼″. Cut each square in half diagonally twice to make 8 triangles (A).

3. From light brown fabric, cut 1 strip 1″ × 20″.

4. From dark brown fabric, cut 1 strip 1″ × 20″.

5. Sew the light brown and dark brown strips together along the longest sides. Press. Use a rotary cutter to crosscut 4 strip pairs 1½″ × 4½″.

6. Following the block assembly diagram for correct placement, sew the strip pairs together along the longest sides, alternating colors. Press.

7. Sew 2 green A triangles to opposite sides of each light beige A triangle. Press.

8. Sew 2 of the triangle trios created in Step 7 to opposite sides of the strip square center. Press. Sew the remaining triangle trios to the other 2 sides. Press.

9. Sew 2 light beige B triangles to opposite sides of the unit created in Step 8. Press. Sew the remaining light beige B triangles to the other 2 sides. Press.

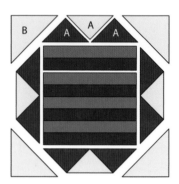

FOND FAREWELL BLOCK D-5

The foundation patterns are on page 112.

1. Make 2 of foundation paper piecing pattern A using red, very light brown, and light beige fabrics.

2. Make 2 of foundation paper piecing pattern B using green and very light brown fabrics.

3. Sew each A foundation to a B foundation to make 2 rows, as shown in the piecing diagram.

4. Sew the rows together.

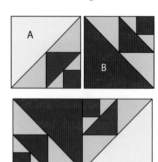

FORT SUMTER

1. From light beige fabric:

- Cut 4 rectangles 1¾″ × 3″ (C).
- Cut 4 squares 1¼″ × 1¼″ (D).
- Cut 2 rectangles 1¼″ × 1¾″ (E).
- Cut 1 rectangle 1¾″ × 3¼″ (F).

2. From red fabric, cut 4 rectangles 1¼″ × 3¼″ (B).

3. From medium blue fabric:

- Cut 2 squares 3⅜″ × 3⅜″. Cut each square in half diagonally twice to make 8 triangles (A).

- Cut 4 squares 1¼″ × 1¼″ (D).

4. Sew 2 medium blue A triangles along a short leg to opposite sides of each light beige C rectangle to make the block corners. Press toward the darker fabric. (*Note:* The excess C fabric will be trimmed after the block is fully assembled.)

5. Sew 2 medium blue D squares to opposite sides of a light beige E rectangle. Press. Repeat to make a second identical unit.

6. Sew the units from Step 5 to opposite sides of the light beige F rectangle. Press.

7. Sew 2 red B rectangles to opposite sides of the unit created in Step 6 as shown in the block assembly diagram. Press.

8. Sew 2 light beige D squares to opposite sides of the 2 remaining red B rectangles. Press.

9. Sew the 2 strips created in Step 8 to opposite sides of the unit created in Step 7 to make the block center. Press.

10. Sew 2 block corners to opposite sides of the central unit. Press. Sew on the other 2 block corners. Press.

11. Square up the block and trim to 6½″ × 6½″ (unfinished size).

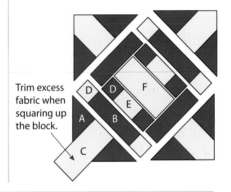

Trim excess fabric when squaring up the block.

FRIENDSHIP KNOT

The template patterns are on page 111.

1. From green fabric, make 4 of template B, adding the appropriate seam allowance for your favorite appliqué method.

2. From light beige fabric:

- Cut 1 square 4¾″ × 4¾″ (A).

- Cut 2 squares 2½″ × 2½″. Cut each square in half diagonally twice to make 8 triangles (D).
- Cut 4 squares 1⅜″ × 1⅜″ (E).
- Cut 4 squares 1¾″ × 1¾″. Cut each square in half diagonally once to make 8 triangles (F).

3. Use template C to make 8 rhombuses from red fabric and 8 from green fabric.

4. Using your favorite method and following the block assembly diagram for placement, appliqué the green B arcs to the light beige A square.

5. Refer to Everett's Oratory (page 37, Steps 10–12) to make 4 block corners with the red and green C rhombuses, light beige D triangles, light beige E squares, and light beige F triangles.

6. Sew 2 block corners to opposite sides of the block center. Press. Sew the remaining block corners to the other sides. Press.

FRIENDSHIP SQUARE

The foundation pattern is on page 113.

Complete the foundation paper piecing pattern using light multi-colored floral fabric for the center square and light brown, medium blue, and light beige fabrics for the triangles. Press. Trim to 6½″ × 6½″ (unfinished).

GERDA'S PUZZLE

Traditional Piecing

1. From red fabric, cut 1 square 3½″ × 3½″ (A) and 2 squares 2⅜″ × 2⅜″ (D).

2. From light beige fabric:

- Cut 1 square 2¾″ × 2¾″. Cut the square in half diagonally twice to make 4 triangles (B).

- Cut 4 squares 2⅜″ × 2⅜″. Cut each square in half diagonally once to make 8 triangles (C).

- Cut 2 squares 2⅜″ × 2⅜″ (D).

3. From light brown fabric, cut 3 squares 2¾″ × 2¾″. Cut each square in half diagonally twice to make 12 triangles (B).

4. Sew each of the 4 light beige B triangles to a light brown

B triangle along the long side. Press. Sew 2 light brown B triangles to the light beige halves of each pair along the short sides. Press. Sew 2 light beige C triangles to each unit. Press.

5. Sew 2 units from Step 4 to opposite sides of the red A square to make the center row. Press.

6. Refer to Quick-Pieced HST Units (page 14, Abel's Favorite, Step 3) to make 4 quick-pieced red and light beige HST units with the D squares.

7. Sew 2 HST units to opposite sides of the remaining units created in Step 4 to make the top and bottom rows. Press.

8. Sew the 3 rows together. Press.

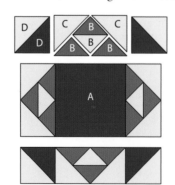

Foundation Paper Piecing

The foundation patterns are on pages 112 and 113.

1. Make 1 of foundation paper piecing pattern A using light beige, light brown, and red fabrics. Press.

2. Make 1 of foundation paper piecing pattern B using light brown and light beige fabrics. Press.

3. Make 2 of foundation paper piecing pattern C using light brown, light beige, and red fabrics. Press.

4. Sew the foundation paper piecing A unit to the foundation paper piecing B unit to make the center row. Press.

5. Sew the 2 foundation paper piecing C units to the top and bottom of the center row. Press.

1. From dark brown fabric, cut 5 squares 2½″ × 2½″ (B) and 4 squares 1½″ × 1½″ (C).

2. From light beige fabric:

- Cut 8 squares 1½″ × 1½″ (A).

- Cut 4 squares 1⅞″ × 1⅞″. Cut each square in half diagonally once to make 8 triangles (D).

3. From light brown fabric, cut 8 squares 1½″ × 1½″ (A).

4. From medium blue fabric:

- Cut 4 squares 1½″ × 1½″ (A).

- Cut 2 squares 2⅞″ × 2⅞″. Cut each square in half diagonally once to make 4 triangles (E).

5. Sew 2 light beige D triangles to adjacent sides of each dark brown C square. Press. Sew a medium blue E triangle to each unit. Press.

6. Refer to Quick-Pieced Square-On-Point Unit (page 14, Abel's Favorite, Step 5) to make 4 quick-pieced square-on-point units, each with 2 light beige A squares, 2 light brown A squares, and 1 dark brown B square, arranging the colors as shown below.

7. Repeat Step 6 with the remaining dark brown B square and the 4 medium blue A squares to make a dark brown and medium blue square-on-point unit.

8. Arrange the block segments into 3 rows and sew. Press. Sew the 3 rows together. Press.

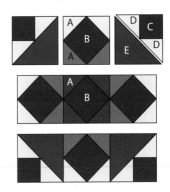

1. From light beige fabric:

- Cut 1 strip 1¼″ × 12″.

- Cut 8 rectangles 1¼″ × 2″ (E).

- Cut 1 square 2¾″ × 2¾″. Cut the square twice diagonally to make 4 triangles (F).

2. From red fabric:

- Cut 1 square 2″ × 2″ (C).

- Cut 8 squares 1¼″ × 1¼″ (B). Draw a diagonal line from corner to corner on the back of each B square.

3. From green fabric:

- Cut 8 rectangles 1¼″ × 3⅛″. Lay the rectangles on a cutting mat in pairs, right sides facing and edges aligned. Use a rotary cutter to trim off a corner of each rectangle pair at a 45° angle to make 4 A and 4 A reverse pieces.

- Cut 4 squares 1¼″ × 1¼″ (B).

- Cut 1 strip 1¼″ × 12″.

4. Sew the green strip and the light beige strip together along the long sides. Press toward the green fabric. Use a rotary cutter to crosscut 8 strips 1¼″ wide. Join the strips in pairs to make 4 Four-Patches.

5. Referring to the block diagram for placement, sew a light beige E rectangle to each Four-Patch. Sew a green B square to the end of each remaining light beige E rectangle. Sew a square/rectangle unit to each Four-Patch unit to create 4 block corners.

6. Place a red B square on the square end of a green A piece, right sides facing and edges aligned. (The drawn line should be parallel to the 45° angle at the top of the A piece.) Sew on the drawn line. Use a rotary cutter to trim the excess fabric ¼″ away from the seam. Repeat to make 4 A/B units and 4 A reverse/B units. Press toward the red fabric for the A units and the green fabric for the A reverse units. Mark the ¼″ seam allowances on the wrong side of each piece.

7. Sewing from point to point only, sew each A/B unit to an A reverse/B unit. Use Y-seam construction to set a light beige F triangle into the angles between the star points. Press. Repeat to make 4 block side units.

8. Sew 2 block side units to opposite sides of the red C square to make the middle row. Press toward the red fabric.

9. Sew 2 block corners to opposite sides of each of the remaining block side units to create the top and bottom rows. Press toward the block corners.

10. Sew the 3 rows together. Press.

The foundation pattern is on page 114.

1. Make 2 of the foundation paper piecing pattern with medium blue and light beige fabrics, as indicated. Make 2 of the foundation paper piecing pattern in the reverse colors. (Swap the light beige for medium blue and vice versa.)

2. Sew the foundations into 2 rows as shown in the block assembly diagram.

3. Sew the rows together.

1. From light beige fabric:

- Cut 2 squares 1⅞″ × 1⅞″ (A).
- Cut 2 rectangles 1⅞″ × 4″ (B).
- Cut 1 square 3¾″ × 3¾″. Cut the square in half diagonally once to make 2 C triangles.

2. From green fabric:

- Cut 2 squares 1⅞″ × 1⅞″ (A).
- Cut 2 rectangles 1⅞″ × 4″ (B).
- Cut 1 square 3¾″ × 3¾″. Cut the square in half diagonally once to make 2 C triangles.

3. Sew a green A square to the end of a light beige B rectangle. Press toward the green fabric. With the right angle of the light beige C triangle aligned with the green A square, sew a light beige C triangle to the right-hand side of the A/B strip. Press toward the A/B strip. Repeat to make a second, identical block quarter. (*Note:* The end of the light beige B rectangle will be trimmed after the block is assembled.)

4. Sew a light beige A square to the end of a green B rectangle. Press toward the green fabric. With the right angle of the green C triangle aligned with the light beige A square, sew a green C triangle to the right-hand side of the A/B strip. Press toward the green C triangle. Repeat to make a second, identical block quarter.

(*Note:* The end of the green B rectangle will be trimmed after the block is assembled.)

5. Sew each light block quarter to a dark block quarter to make 2 block halves. Press.

6. Sew the block halves together. Press. Trim the block to 6½″ × 6½″ unfinished.

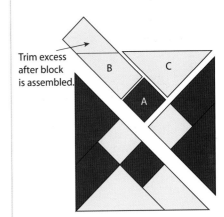

Trim excess after block is assembled.

GUIDING STAR

The template patterns are on page 114.

1. From red fabric, make 4 kites using template A.

2. From medium blue fabric, make 4 triangles using template B and 4 triangles using template C.

3. From light beige fabric:

- Make 4 triangles using template D. Flip the template and make 4 D reverse triangles.

- Make 4 using template E. Flip the template and make 4 E reverses.

- Make 4 kites using template F.

4. Sew a light beige D and a light beige D reverse to each red A to make 4 block corners. Press.

5. Sew a light beige E and a light beige E reverse to each medium blue B to make 4 block sides. Press.

6. Sew a light beige F to a medium blue C triangle. Press. Repeat to make 4.

7. Sew 2 units created in Step 6 together. Press. Repeat with the remaining units.

8. Sew the units created in Step 7 together to make the block center. Press.

9. Following the block assembly diagram, sew the segments into 3 rows. Press. Sew the rows together. Press.

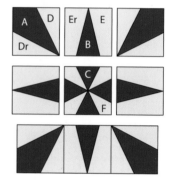

HAPPY HOME

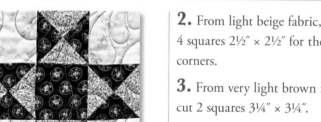

1. From dark blue fabric:

- Cut 2 squares 3¼″ × 3¼″.

- Cut 1 square 2½″ × 2½″ for the center of the block.

2. From light beige fabric, cut 4 squares 2½″ × 2½″ for the block corners.

3. From very light brown fabric, cut 2 squares 3¼″ × 3¼″.

4. Refer to Quick-Pieced QST Units (page 27, Combination Star, Step 5) to make 4 quick-pieced quarter-square triangle units with the very light brown and dark blue 3¼″ × 3¼″ squares.

5. Sew the segments into 3 rows as shown in the block assembly diagram. Press. Sew the 3 rows together. Press.

The template patterns are on pages 114 and 115.

1. From light beige fabric, make 4 hexagons using template A.

2. From light brown fabric:

- Cut 4 squares 1⅝″ × 1⅝″. Cut each square in half diagonally once to make 8 triangles (B).

- Make 4 triangles using template C.

3. From dark brown fabric:

- Cut 2 squares 1⅝″ × 1⅝″. Cut each square in half diagonally once to make 4 triangles (B).

- Make 4 kites using template D.

4. From red fabric, cut 2 squares 3⅛″ × 3⅛″. Cut each square in half diagonally once to make 4 triangles (E).

5. Sew a dark brown D kite to a light brown C triangle. Press. Repeat to make 4.

6. Sew the units from Step 5 together in pairs. Press. Sew the pairs together to make the block center. Press.

7. Following the block assembly diagram, sew 2 light brown B triangles to 2 short sides of each light beige A hexagon. Press.

8. Sew 2 units created in Step 7 to opposite sides of the block center. Press.

9. Sew 2 dark brown B triangles to the light brown B triangles of the remaining units created in Step 7. Press.

10. Sew the units created in Step 9 to the remaining sides of the block center. Press.

11. Sew 2 red E triangles to opposite sides of the unit created in Step 10. Press. Sew on the remaining red E triangles. Press.

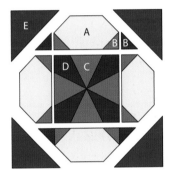

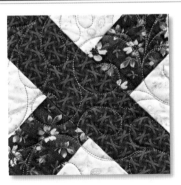

1. From light beige fabric, cut 1 square 4¼″ × 4¼″. Cut the square in half diagonally twice to make 4 triangles (A).

2. From medium blue fabric, cut 2 rectangles 2⅝″ × 5″ (B).

3. From green fabric, cut 1 rectangle 2⅝″ × 9¾″ (C). Fold in half widthwise and press with a hot iron to mark the center.

4. Aligning a short leg with the edge, sew 2 light beige A triangles to opposite sides of each medium blue B strip. Fold in half through the A/B/A side and press with a hot iron to mark the center.

5. Sew the units created in Step 4 to opposite sides of the C strip, aligning the center creases. Press.

6. Trim the excess medium blue and green fabric so the block measures 6½″ × 6½″ (for a finished size of 6″ × 6″).

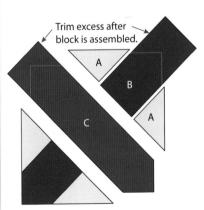

Trim excess after block is assembled.

1. From light beige fabric:

- Cut 4 squares 1⅞″ × 1⅞″. Cut each square in half diagonally once to make 8 triangles (A).

- Cut 1 square 3¼″ × 3¼″. Cut the square in half diagonally twice to make 4 triangles (B).

- Cut 1 square 4½″ × 4½″ (E).

2. From light brown fabric, cut 4 squares 2½″ × 2½″ (C).

3. From dark blue fabric:

- Cut 2 squares 3¼″ × 3¼″. Cut the square in half diagonally twice to make 8 triangles (B).

- Cut 4 squares 1½″ × 1½″ (D).

4. Refer to Quick-Pieced Square-On-Point Unit (page 14, Abel's Favorite, Step 5) to make a quick-pieced square-on-point unit with the 4 light brown C squares and 1 light beige E square.

5. Sew 2 dark blue B triangles to the short sides of each light beige B triangle. Press. Sew a light beige A triangle to each end of the B units. Press.

6. Referring to the block diagram for color placement, sew 2 of the units created in Step 5 to opposite sides of the square-on-point unit created in Step 4 to make the center row. Press toward the E square.

7. Sew 2 dark blue D squares to opposite ends of each remaining unit created in Step 5 to make the top and bottom rows. Press toward the dark blue D squares.

8. Sew the 3 rows together. Press.

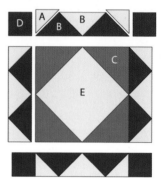

The template patterns are on page 115.

1. From light beige fabric:

- Cut 2 rectangles 1¾″ × 4″ (A).

- Cut 2 rectangles 1¾″ × 6½″ (B).

- Make 4 squares using template C.

2. From red fabric, cut 5 squares using template C.

3. From light brown fabric, make 12 of template D, adding the appropriate seam allowance for your preferred appliqué method.

4. Sew 2 red C squares to opposite sides of a light beige C square. Press toward the red fabric. Repeat to make an identical unit. Sew 2 light beige C squares to opposite sides of the remaining red C square. Press toward the red fabric. Sew the 3 rows together to make the central Nine-Patch.

5. Sew the 2 light beige A rectangles to opposite sides of the central Nine-Patch. Press. Sew the 2 light beige B rectangles to the top and bottom. Press.

6. Using your preferred method and following the block assembly diagram for placement, appliqué the 12 D pieces in place.

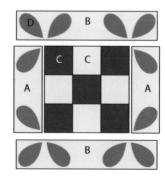

1. From light beige fabric, cut 3 squares 2⅞″ × 2⅞″ (A). Cut 2 of the squares in half diagonally once to make 4 triangles (B).

2. From medium blue fabric, cut 1 square 4⅞″ × 4⅞″. Cut the square in half diagonally once to make 2 triangles (C).

3. From light brown fabric, cut 1 square 2⅞″ × 2⅞″ (A) and 1 square 2½″ × 2½″ (D).

4. Refer to Quick-Pieced HST Units (page 14, Abel's Favorite, Step 3) to make 2 HST units with a light beige and a light brown A square.

5. Sew a light beige B triangle to a light brown edge of each HST unit. Press.

6. Sew 2 light beige B triangles to opposite sides of the light brown D square. Press.

7. Sew the units created in Step 5 to the unit created in Step 6. Press.

8. Sew the 2 medium blue C triangles to opposite sides of the unit created in Step 7. Press.

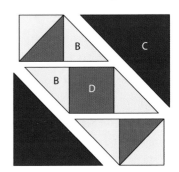

1. From light beige fabric, cut 1 square 2½″ × 2½″ (A), 2 squares 3¼″ × 3¼″ (C), and 2 squares 2⅞″ × 2⅞″ (E).

2. From green fabric, cut 4 squares 1½″ × 1½″ (B), 8 squares 1⅞″ × 1⅞″ (D), and 2 squares 2⅞″ × 2⅞″ (E).

3. Refer to Quick-Pieced Square-On-Point Unit (page 14, Abel's Favorite, Step 5) to make a square-on-point unit with 4 green B squares and the light beige A square.

4. Refer to Quick-Pieced Flying Geese Units (page 14, Abel's Favorite, Step 4) to make 8 Flying Geese units from 8 green D squares and 2 light beige C squares.

5. Sew the Flying Geese units together in 4 pairs.

6. Refer to Quick-Pieced HST Units (page 14, Abel's Favorite, Step 3) to make 4 quick-pieced HST units from 2 green and 2 light beige E squares.

7. Arrange the block segments into 3 rows as shown. Sew the segments together. Press. Sew the 3 rows together. Press.

IMPROVED FOUR-PATCH

The template pattern is on page 115.

1. From light beige fabric, cut 2 squares 3⅞″ × 3⅞″. Cut each square in half diagonally once to make 4 triangles (A).

2. From red fabric, cut 2 squares 2⅝″ × 2⅝″ (B) and 4 squares from template C.

3. From medium blue fabric, cut 4 squares from template C.

4. Sew each red C square to a medium blue C square. Press toward the red squares. Sew these units together in pairs with seams abutted and red squares facing blue squares to make 2 Four-Patches. Press.

5. Sew each Four-Patch to a red B square as shown. Press.

6. Sew these units together in pairs with seams abutted and red B squares facing Four-Patches. Press.

7. Sew 2 light beige A triangles to opposite sides of the unit created in Step 6. Press. Sew the remaining 2 light beige A triangles to the other 2 sides. Press.

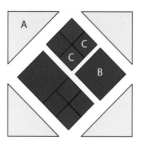

INDIANA

1. From green fabric, cut 5 squares 2½″ × 2½″ (A).

2. From light beige fabric, cut 2 squares 2⅞″ × 2⅞″ (C) and 20 squares 1½″ × 1½″ (B).

3. From red fabric, cut 2 squares 2⅞″ × 2⅞″ (C).

4. Refer to Quick-Pieced Square-On-Point Unit (page 14, Abel's Favorite, Step 5) to make 5 quick-pieced square-on-point units from 5 green A squares and 20 light beige B squares.

5. Refer to Quick-Pieced HST Units (page 14, Abel's Favorite, Step 3) to make 4 quick-pieced HST units from 2 red and 2 light beige C squares.

6. Sew 3 of the square-on-point units created in Step 4 together to make the center row. Press.

7. Sew 2 HST units to opposite sides of the remaining square-on-point unit to make the top row. Press. Repeat to make the bottom row.

8. Sew the 3 rows together. Press.

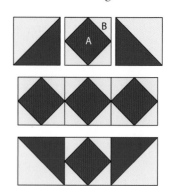

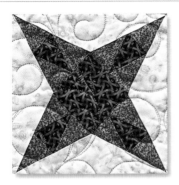

Traditional Piecing

The template patterns are on page 115.

1. From light beige fabric, make 4 triangles using template A.

2. From light brown fabric, make 12 triangles using template B.

3. From medium blue fabric, make 4 triangles using template B and cut 1 square 2⅝" × 2⅝" (C).

4. Sew 2 light brown B triangles to the long sides of each medium blue B triangle. Press. Sew another light brown B triangle to the top of each unit to make 4 star points. Press.

5. Sewing from point to point only and not into the seam allowances, sew 2 star points to opposite sides of the medium blue C square. Press. Sew the remaining star points to the other 2 sides, again sewing from point to point only. Press.

6. Sewing from point to point only, sew the 4 light beige A triangles to adjacent star points, pressing after each addition. Sew in the order and direction shown.

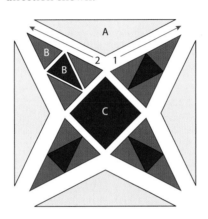

Foundation Paper Piecing

The foundation pattern is on page 116.

1. Using medium blue, light brown, and light beige fabrics, make 4 of the Iowa Star foundation paper piecing pattern. Press.

2. Sew the foundations into 2 rows as shown. Press.

3. Sew the rows together. Press.

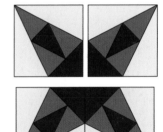

1. From light beige fabric, cut 2 strips 1¼″ × 12″ and 4 squares 2⅜″ × 2⅜″ (A).

2. From red fabric, cut 1 strip 1¼″ × 12″ and 2 squares 2⅜″ × 2⅜″ (A).

3. From dark brown fabric, cut 1 strip 1¼″ × 12″ and 2 squares 2⅜″ × 2⅜″ (A).

4. Sew the dark brown strip and a light beige strip together along the longest side. Press toward the dark brown fabric. Crosscut 8 strips 1¼″ wide. Repeat this step with the second light beige strip and the red strip.

5. Pair each dark brown / light beige crosscut strip with a red / light beige crosscut strip. With dark fabrics facing light and seams abutted, sew the strips together to make 8 Four-Patches.

6. Refer to Quick-Pieced HST Units (page 14, Abel's Favorite, Step 3) to make 4 HST units from 2 red and 2 light beige A squares.

7. Repeat Step 6 to make 4 more HST units, but this time from 2 dark brown and 2 light beige A squares.

8. Arrange the block segments as shown in the block assembly diagram. Sew into 4 rows. Press alternate rows in opposite directions.

9. Sew the 4 rows together. Press seams open to reduce bulk.

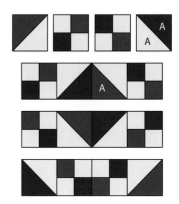

JONATHAN'S SATCHEL

1. From light brown fabric, cut 1 square 4½″ × 4½″ (A).

2. From light beige fabric, cut 2 squares 2⅞″ × 2⅞″. Cut each square in half diagonally once to make 4 triangles (B).

3. Cut 1 strip 1″ × 12″ from light beige fabric and 1 strip 1″ × 12″ from medium blue fabric.

4. From medium blue fabric, cut 4 squares 1⅞″ × 1⅞″. Cut each square in half diagonally once to make 8 triangles (C).

5. Sew the medium blue strip and the light beige strip together along the longest side. Press toward the medium blue fabric. Crosscut 4 strips 1½″ × 2½″.

6. Sew 2 medium blue C triangles to opposite ends of each crosscut strip. Press.

7. Sew 2 units created in Step 6 to opposite sides of the light brown A square. Press. Sew the remaining units to the other 2 sides. Press.

8. Sew 2 light beige B triangles to opposite sides of the unit created in Step 7. Press. Sew on the other 2 light beige B triangles. Press.

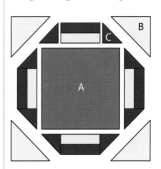

KANSAS STAR

1. From light brown fabric, cut 4 squares 2½″ × 2½″ (A).

2. From light beige fabric, cut 20 squares 1½″ × 1½″ (B).

3. From green fabric, cut 5 squares 2½″ × 2½″ (A) and 16 squares 1½″ × 1½″ (B).

4. Refer to Quick-Pieced Square-On-Point Unit (page 14, Abel's Favorite, Step 5) to make 5 quick-pieced square-on-point units from 20 light beige B squares and 5 green A squares.

5. Repeat Step 4 to make 4 more square-on-point units, but this time from 16 green B squares and 4 light brown A squares.

6. Arrange the block segments into 3 rows and sew. Press alternate rows in opposite directions. Sew the 3 rows together. Press seams open to reduce bulk.

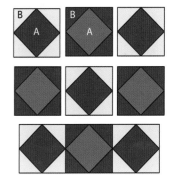

The template pattern is on page 114.
The foundation patterns are on page 116.

1. From light beige fabric:

- Cut 2 squares 2⅜" × 2⅜". Cut each square in half diagonally once to make 4 triangles (A).

- Cut 1 square 4¼" × 4¼". Cut the square in half diagonally twice to make 4 triangles (B).

2. Using template C, make 4 squares from medium blue fabric and 5 squares from very light brown fabric.

3. Sew 2 very light brown C squares to opposite sides of a medium blue C square. Press toward the medium blue square. Repeat to make an identical row. Sew 2 medium blue C squares to opposite sides of a very light brown C square. Press toward the medium blue squares. Sew the 3 rows together to make the central Nine-Patch.

4. Make 4 of foundation paper piecing pattern D. Make 4 of foundation paper piecing pattern E.

5. Pair each D with an E and sew together. Press.

6. Sew 2 of the D/E foundation units to opposite sides of the central Nine-Patch. Press.

7. Sew 2 light beige B triangles to opposite sides of each remaining D/E foundation unit. Press.

8. Sew the units created in Step 7 to opposite sides of the unit created in Step 6. Press.

9. Sew the light beige A triangles to the corners of the block. Press.

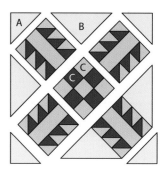

LADIES AID BLOCK

The template pattern is on page 106.

1. Use template A to make 2 squares from red fabric and 2 squares from medium blue.

2. From red fabric:

- Cut 1 square 1⅞″ × 1⅞″. Cut the square in half diagonally once to make 2 triangles (B). Repeat this step with medium blue fabric to make 2 triangles (B).

- Cut 1 square 3⅞″ × 3⅞″. Cut the square in half diagonally once to make 2 triangles (D). Repeat this step with medium blue fabric to make 2 triangles (D).

3. From light beige fabric, cut 2 squares 3¼″ × 3¼″. Cut each square in half diagonally twice to make 8 triangles (C).

4. Sew 2 light beige C triangles to opposite sides of each A square. Press.

5. Sew a medium blue B triangle to each red A square. Press. Sew a red B triangle to each medium blue A square. Press.

6. Sew a medium blue D triangle to each medium blue A unit. Press.

Sew a red D triangle to each red A unit. Press.

7. Sew the block quarters into 2 rows as shown. Press toward the red D triangles.

8. Sew the 2 rows together. Press.

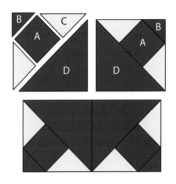

LIBBY PRISON

1. From dark brown fabric, cut 1 strip 1¼″ × 12″ and 2 squares 2⅞″ × 2⅞″ (A).

2. From light beige fabric, cut 2 strips 1⅛″ × 12″ and 2 squares 2⅞″ × 2⅞″ (A).

3. From light brown fabric, cut 1 square 2½″ × 2½″.

4. Sew the 2 light beige strips to opposite sides of the dark brown strip. Press toward the dark brown fabric. Use a rotary cutter to crosscut 4 units 2½″ wide.

5. Refer to Quick-Pieced HST Units (page 14, Abel's Favorite, Step 3) to make 4 HST units from 2 dark brown and 2 light beige A squares.

6. Sew 2 of the units created in Step 4 to opposite sides of the light brown square as shown to make the center row. Press toward the light brown square.

7. Sew 2 HST units to opposite sides of a unit created in Step 4 as shown to make the top row. Press toward the HST units. Repeat this step to make the bottom row.

8. Sew the 3 rows together. Press.

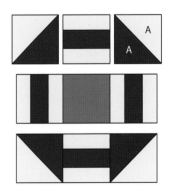

The template patterns are on page 116.

1. From light beige fabric, make 12 triangles using template A, 4 triangles using template B, and 4 rectangles using template C.

2. From medium blue fabric, make 4 rectangles using template C.

3. From red fabric, make 4 rectangles using template D.

4. From dark brown fabric, make 4 squares using template E and 1 square using template F.

5. Sew 2 dark brown E squares to opposite sides of a light beige C rectangle. Press toward the dark brown fabric. Repeat to make an identical row. Sew 2 light beige C rectangles to opposite sides of the dark brown F square. Press toward the dark brown fabric. Sew the 3 rows together to make an asymmetric Nine-Patch. Press.

6. Sew 2 light beige A triangles to opposite ends of each medium blue C rectangle. Press. Sew a light beige B triangle to the top of each unit. Press. Sew a red D rectangle to the bottom of each unit to make 4 block corners. Press.

7. Sew 2 block corners to opposite sides of the asymmetric Nine-Patch. Press.

8. Sew 2 light beige A triangles to opposite ends of the red rectangle on each remaining block corner. Press.

9. Sew the remaining block corners to the other sides of the asymmetric Nine-Patch. Press.

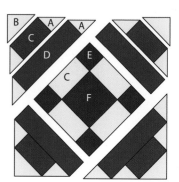

LOST CHILDREN

The template patterns are on pages 116 and 117.

1. From light beige fabric, cut 1 square 2⅝″ × 2⅝″ (C) and make 4 triangles using template A.

2. Using template B, make 12 triangles from very light brown fabric and 24 triangles from red fabric.

3. Sew 3 red B triangles to 2 very light brown B triangles, alternating colors and forming the bottom row of a star point. Press. Repeat to make 4.

4. Sew 2 red B triangles to the long sides of each remaining very light brown B triangle. Press. Sew another red B triangle to the top of each unit. Press.

5. Sew each unit created in Step 3 to a unit created in Step 4 to make 4 star points. Press.

6. Sewing from point to point only and not into the seam allowances, sew 2 star points to opposite sides of the light beige C square. Press.

Sew the remaining star points to the other 2 sides, again sewing from point to point only. Press.

7. Sewing from point to point only and not into the seam allowances, add the 4 light beige A triangles to adjacent star points.

MAINE

The template pattern is on page 115.

1. From light beige fabric:

- Cut 1 square 3¼″ × 3¼″. Cut the square in half diagonally twice to make 4 triangles (A).

- Cut 4 squares 2½″ × 2½″ (C).

2. From light brown fabric, cut 1 strip 1⅛″ × 12″.

3. From medium blue fabric:

- Cut 2 squares 3¼″ × 3¼″. Cut the squares in half diagonally twice to make 8 triangles (A).

- Make 1 square using template B.

4. Sew the light brown strip to one side of the medium blue B square. Press and trim the strip even with the square. Repeat for the opposite side of the square. Sew the strip to an adjacent side, press, and trim the strip even with the shorter strips. Repeat for the opposite side.

5. Sew 2 medium blue A triangles to adjacent sides of each light beige C square. Press.

6. Sew 2 units created in Step 5 to opposite sides of the unit created in Step 4. Press.

7. Sew 2 light beige A triangles to the remaining 2 units created in Step 5. Press.

8. Sew the units created in Step 7 to opposite sides of the block. Press.

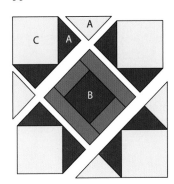

1. From light beige fabric, cut 2 strips 1½″ × 8″ and 8 squares 1½″ × 1½″ (A).

2. From dark blue fabric, cut 1 strip 1½″ × 8″ and 4 squares 2½″ × 2½″ (B).

3. From red fabric, cut 1 strip 1½″ × 8″ and 1 square 2½″ × 2½″ (C).

4. Sew the dark blue strip and a light beige strip together along the longest side. Press toward the dark blue fabric. Crosscut 4 strips 1½″ wide. Repeat with the second light beige strip and the red strip.

5. Pair each dark blue / light beige crosscut strip with a red / light beige crosscut strip. With darker fabrics facing light and seams abutted, sew the strips together to make 4 Four-Patches. Press.

6. Refer to Quick-Pieced Square-On-Point Unit (page 14, Abel's Favorite, Step 5, a–d *only*) to sew 2 light beige A squares to each dark blue B square as shown.

7. Arrange the block segments as shown in the block assembly diagram and sew into 3 rows. Press.

8. Sew the 3 rows together. Press.

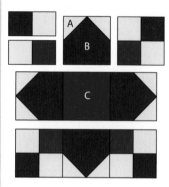

1. From light beige fabric:

- Cut 4 squares 1⅞" × 1⅞". Cut each square in half diagonally once to make 8 triangles (C).

- Cut 1 square 3¼" × 3¼". Cut the square in half diagonally twice to make 4 triangles (D).

- Cut 2 squares 2⅞" × 2⅞". Cut each square once diagonally to make 4 triangles (E).

2. From red fabric, cut 1 square 2½" × 2½" (B) and 4 rectangles 1¼" × 4". Cut 45° triangles from both ends of each rectangle to make 4 trapezoids (A).

3. From dark brown fabric, cut 4 rectangles 1¼" × 4¾".

4. Sew 2 light beige D triangles to opposite sides of the red B square. Press. Sew the remaining light beige D triangles to the other 2 sides. Press.

5. Sew 2 of the dark brown strips to opposite sides of the central square unit from Step 4. Press and trim the edges even. Center and sew the remaining dark brown strips to the top and bottom of the central unit. Press and trim the edges even. The unit should measure 4¾" × 4¾".

6. Sew a light beige C triangle to each diagonal side of a red A trapezoid. Sew a light beige E triangle to the longest side of the trapezoid to make a corner unit. Press. Repeat to make 4 corner units.

7. Sew 2 corner units to opposite sides of the central square unit. Press. Sew the remaining corner units to the other 2 opposite sides. Press.

The template patterns are on page 117.

1. From light beige fabric, cut 10 squares 1⅞″ × 1⅞″ (D) and 1 square using template E.

2. Cut 8 D squares in half diagonally once to make 16 triangles (A).

3. From green fabric, make 4 parallelograms using template B. Flip the template and make 4 B reverse.

4. From medium blue fabric, cut 2 squares 2⅞″ × 2⅞″. Cut each square in half diagonally once to make 4 triangles (C).

5. Sew a light beige A triangle to each B and B reverse as shown. Press.

6. Refer to Quick-Pieced HST Units (page 14, Abel's Favorite, Step 3) to make 4 HST units from 2 light beige and 2 medium blue D squares.

7. Sew 2 light beige A triangles to each HST unit as shown. Press. Sew a medium blue C triangle to each unit. Press.

8. Sew 1 B and 1 B reverse unit as shown to each of the units created in Step 7 to make the block corners. Press.

9. Sewing from point to point only and not into the seam allowances, sew 2 of the block corners to opposite sides of the light beige E square.

10. Again sewing from point to point only, sew on the other 2 block corners following the order and direction shown. Press.

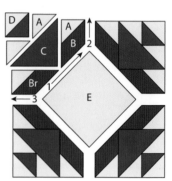

Traditional Piecing

1. From light beige fabric, cut 2 squares 3½″ × 3½″ (A) and 8 squares 2″ × 2″ (B).

2. From medium brown fabric, cut 2 squares 3½″ × 3½″ (A) and 8 squares 2″ × 2″ (B).

3. Refer to Quick-Pieced Square-On-Point Unit (page 14, Abel's Favorite, Step 5) to make 2 quick-pieced square-on-point units from the 2 light beige A squares and the 8 medium brown B squares.

4. Repeat Step 3 to make 2 more quick-pieced square-on-point units, this time with the colors reversed, from the 2 medium brown A squares and the 8 light beige B squares.

5. Sew the units into 2 rows. Press.

6. Sew the rows together. Press.

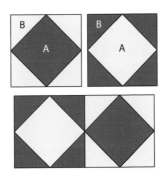

Foundation Paper Piecing

The foundation pattern is on page 117.

1. Using medium brown and light beige fabrics, make 2 of the foundation paper piecing pattern, placing the colors where indicated.

2. Make 2 of the foundation paper piecing pattern in the reverse colors (swap the light beige for medium brown and vice versa).

3. Sew the foundations into 2 rows as shown (at left). Press.

4. Sew the rows together. Press.

1. From light beige fabric:

- Cut 8 squares 1½″ × 1½″ (A) and 4 squares 1⅞″ × 1⅞″ (C).

- Cut 1 square 3¼″ × 3¼″. Cut the square in half twice diagonally to make 4 triangles (B).

2. From red fabric:

- Cut 8 rectangles 1½″ × 2⅞″ (D). Place the rectangles on a cutting mat in pairs, right sides facing and edges aligned. Use a rotary cutter to trim off a corner of each rectangle pair at a 45° angle to make 4 D's and 4 D reverses.

- Cut 1 square 2½″ × 2½″ (E).

3. From medium blue fabric, cut 4 squares 1⅞″ × 1⅞″ (C) and 8 squares 1½″ × 1½″ (F). Draw a diagonal line from corner to corner on the back of each F square.

4. Place a medium blue F square on the square end of a red D piece, right sides facing and edges aligned as shown below. Sew on the drawn line. Trim the excess fabric ¼″ away from the seam. Press toward the medium blue fabric. Repeat to make 4 D/F units and 4 D reverse/F units. Mark the ¼″ seam allowances on the wrong side of each piece.

5. Sewing from point to point only and not into the seam allowances, sew each D/F unit to a D reverse/F unit. Again sewing from point to point only and not into the seam allowances, sew a light beige B triangle into the angles between the star points. Press. Repeat to make 4 block side units.

6. Refer to Quick-Pieced HST Units (page 14, Abel's Favorite, Step 3) to make 8 quick-pieced HST units from 4 light beige and 5 medium blue C squares.

7. Sew a light beige A square to each HST unit as shown. Press toward the HST unit. Sew the units together in pairs to make 4 block corners. Press.

8. Sew 2 of the block side units created in Step 5 to opposite sides of the red E square to make the center row. Press toward the E square.

9. Sew 2 block corners to opposite sides of another block side unit to make the top row. Press toward the block corners. Repeat to make the bottom row.

10. Sew the 3 rows together. Press.

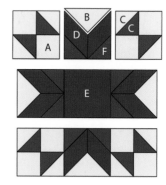

The template pattern is on page 118.

1. From light beige fabric:

- Cut 2 squares $2\frac{7}{8}'' \times 2\frac{7}{8}''$. Cut each square in half diagonally to make 4 triangles (A).

- Cut 1 square $2\frac{1}{2}'' \times 2\frac{1}{2}''$ (B).

2. Using template C, make 2 hexagons from light brown fabric and 2 from medium blue fabric.

3. Sewing from point to point only and not into the seam allowances, sew a light brown C hexagon to one side of the light beige B square and sew a medium blue C hexagon to the opposite side, as shown.

4. Sewing point to point only and following the order and direction shown, sew a light brown C hexagon and a medium blue C hexagon to the remaining sides of the light beige B square and to the adjacent hexagons. Press.

5. Sew the light beige A triangles to the corners of the block. Press.

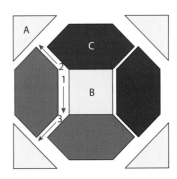

The template pattern is on page 115.

1. Using template A, make 8 rhombuses from light brown fabric and 8 from green fabric.

2. From light beige fabric:

- Cut 2 squares 3″ × 3″. Cut each square in half diagonally twice to make 8 triangles (B).

- Cut 4 squares 1¾″ × 1¾″ (C) and 1 square 3″ × 3″ (D).

3. Sewing from point to point only and not into the seam allowances, sew each light brown A rhombus to a green A rhombus. Press. Make 4 pairs and 4 mirror-image pairs as shown.

4. Sewing from point to point only, sew a light beige B triangle to each light brown / green A rhombus pair and mirror-image pair. Press.

5. Referring to the block diagram and sewing from point to point only, sew 1 light beige C square to 4 identical A/A/B units. Press. Sew each of these units to a mirror-image A/A/B unit. Press. Make 4 block corners.

6. Sewing from point to point only, sew 2 block corners to opposite sides of the light beige D square. Press. Again sewing from point to point only, sew the remaining block corners to the other sides. Follow the seam order and direction shown. Press.

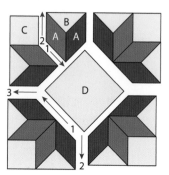

The foundation pattern is on page 118.

1. Make 4 of the foundation paper piecing pattern using medium blue, light brown, red, and light beige fabrics. Press.

2. Sew the foundations into 2 rows as shown. Press.

3. Sew the rows together. Press.

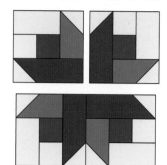

The template patterns are on page 117.

1. From medium blue fabric, make 8 rhombuses using template A.

2. From light beige fabric:

- Cut 2 squares 3″ × 3″. Cut each square in half diagonally twice to make 8 triangles (B). Mark ¼″ seam allowances on the back of the fabric.

- Cut 2 squares 2½″ × 2½″. Cut each square in half diagonally twice to make 8 triangles (D). Mark ¼″ seam allowances on the back of the fabric.

- Cut 4 squares 1⅜″ × 1⅜″ (E) and 4 rectangles 1⅜″ × 2¼″ (F).

3. From red fabric, make 16 rhombuses using template C.

4. Sewing from point to point only and not into the seam allowances, sew the medium blue A rhombuses together in pairs. Press.

5. Sewing from point to point only and not into the seam allowances, sew a light beige B triangle to each medium blue A rhombus pair. Press. Make 4.

6. Sewing from point to point only, sew a light beige B triangle as shown to each unit created in Step 5. Press.

7. Sewing from point to point only, sew the units created in Step 6 into pairs. Press. Sew the pairs together in the order and direction shown. Press.

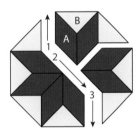

8. Sewing from point to point only, sew 2 light beige F rectangles to opposite sides of the unit created in Step 7. Press. Sew 2 light beige F rectangles to the other 2 sides. Press.

9. Sewing from point to point only, sew the red C rhombuses together in pairs. Press. Repeat to make 8 pairs.

10. Sewing from point to point only, sew a light beige D triangle to each pair created in Step 9. Press.

11. Sewing from point to point only, sew a light beige E square as shown to a unit created in Step 10. Press. Repeat to make 4. Sew each of these units to a unit without a light beige E square to make 4 block corners. Press.

12. Sewing from point to point only and in the order and direction shown, sew block corners to the corners of the block center. Press.

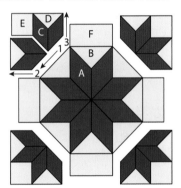

1. From light beige fabric:

- Cut 4 squares 2″ × 2″ (A) and 1 square 3½″ × 3½″ (C).

- Cut 1 square 4¼″ × 4¼″. Cut the square in half diagonally twice to make 4 triangles (B).

2. From light brown fabric, cut 2 squares 2¾″ × 2¾″. Cut each square in half diagonally twice to make 8 triangles (D).

3. From dark brown fabric:

- Cut 2 squares 2¾″ × 2¾″. Cut each square in half diagonally twice to make 8 triangles (D).

- Cut 4 squares 2″ × 2″ (E).

4. Refer to Quick-Pieced Square-On-Point Unit (page 14, Abel's Favorite, Step 5) to make a quick-pieced square-on-point unit from the light beige C square and the 4 dark brown E squares.

5. Sew each dark brown D triangle to a light brown D triangle as shown. Press. Make 4 pairs and 4 mirror-image pairs.

6. Sew a D/D triangle pair and a D/D mirror-image pair to each light beige B triangle. Press.

7. Sew 2 of the units created in Step 6 to opposite sides of the block center to make the center row. Press toward the block center.

8. Sew 2 light beige A squares to opposite sides of a unit created in Step 6 to make the top row. Press toward the A squares. Repeat to make the bottom row. Press.

9. Sew the 3 rows together. Press.

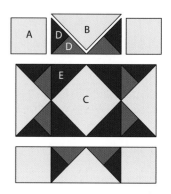

The template pattern is on page 118.

1. From light beige fabric:

- Cut 4 squares 2⅛″ × 2⅛″. Cut each square in half diagonally once to make 8 triangles (A).

- Cut 4 rectangles 1½″ × 3″ (B).

2. From light brown fabric, cut 1 square 1½″ × 1½″ (C) and 4 squares 1¾″ × 1¾″ (D).

3. Using template E, make 4 parallelograms from dark brown fabric. Flip the template and make 4 E reverse parallelograms from red fabric.

4. Sewing from point to point only and not into the seam allowances, sew each dark brown E to a red E reverse.

5. Sewing from point to point only, sew a light brown D square to each E/E reverse pair. Press.

6. Sew 2 light beige A triangles to each unit created in Step 5. Press.

7. Sew 2 units created in Step 6 to opposite sides of a light beige B rectangle to make the top row.

Press toward the B rectangle. Repeat to make the bottom row.

8. Sew 2 light beige B rectangles to opposite sides of the light brown C square to make the center row. Press toward the B rectangles.

9. Sew the 3 rows together. Press.

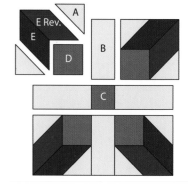

The template patterns are on pages 118 and 119.

1. Using template A, make 4 from light beige fabric and 4 from medium blue fabric.

2. Using template B, make 4 from medium blue fabric. Flip the template and make 4 B reverse from light beige fabric. (*Note:* Trace templates on the *wrong* side of the fabric.)

3. From light beige fabric:

- Cut 2 squares 1⅝" × 1⅝". Cut each square in half diagonally once to make 4 triangles (C). Repeat with medium blue fabric.

- Cut 1 square 2¾" × 2¾". Cut the square in half diagonally twice to make 4 triangles (D). Repeat with medium blue fabric.

4. Sew each medium blue A to a light beige D triangle as shown to make 4 A/D units. Sew each light beige A to a medium blue D triangle to make 4 opposite A/D units. Press toward the medium blue fabric.

5. Sew each A/D unit to an opposite A/D unit. Press toward the opposite A/D unit. Make 4.

6. Sew each light beige C triangle to a medium blue B to make 4 B/C units. Sew each medium blue C triangle to a light beige B reverse to make 4 reverse B/C units. Press toward the medium blue fabric.

7. Sew each B/C unit to a reverse B/C unit. Press toward the B/C unit. Make 4.

8. Sew each unit made in Step 5 to a unit made in Step 7 to make 4 block quarters. Press. Sew the block quarters into 2 rows. Press. Sew the rows together. Press.

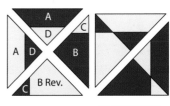

The template patterns are on page 118.

1. From light beige fabric:

■ Cut 4 squares 1⅜″ × 1⅜″. Cut each square in half diagonally once to make 8 triangles (A).

■ Make 4 pentagons using template B and 4 pentagons using template C.

■ Cut 2 squares 2⅞″ × 2⅞″. Cut each square in half diagonally once to make 4 triangles (E).

2. From red fabric:

■ Make 1 square using template D.

■ Cut 1 square 2¼″ × 2¼″. Cut the square in half diagonally twice to make 4 triangles (F).

■ Cut 2 squares 2¾″ × 2¾″. Cut each square in half diagonally twice to make 8 triangles (G).

3. From light brown fabric, make 4 pentagons using template H.

4. Sew 2 light beige A triangles to each light brown H pentagon as shown. Press.

5. Sew 2 red G triangles to each light beige C pentagon. Press. Sew a light beige E triangle to each unit to make 4 block corners. Press.

6. Sew 2 light beige B pentagons to opposite sides of the red D square. Press.

7. Sew 2 red F triangles to opposite sides of each remaining light beige B pentagon. Press.

8. Sew the units created in Step 7 to opposite sides of the unit created in Step 6 to make the block center. Press.

9. Sew 2 units from Step 4 to opposite sides of the block center to make the middle row. Press.

10. Sew 2 block corners to opposite sides of a unit from Step 4 to make the top row. Press. Repeat to make the bottom row.

11. Sew the 3 rows together. Press.

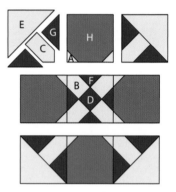

NEW YORK STATE

The template patterns are on page 119.

1. From light beige fabric:

- Cut 2 squares 2⅝″ × 2⅝″. Cut each square in half diagonally once to make 4 triangles (A).

- Make 8 triangles using template B.

2. From light brown fabric, make 4 triangles using template B.

3. From medium blue fabric, make 4 trapezoids using template C.

4. From dark brown fabric, make 4 rhombuses using template D.

5. Sew 2 light beige B triangles to each dark brown D rhombus as shown. Press.

6. Sew a light brown B triangle to each medium blue C trapezoid. Sew a light beige A triangle to the opposite side of the trapezoid. Press.

7. Sew each unit created in Step 5 to a unit created in Step 6 to make a block quarter. Press.

8. Sew the block quarters together in pairs. Press.

9. Sew the pairs together. Press.

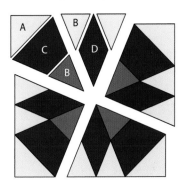

NORTH STAR

The template patterns are on page 119.

1. From light beige fabric, make 4 of template A. Flip the template and make 4 A reverse.

2. Using template B, make 4 kites from green fabric and 4 from medium blue fabric.

3. Using template C, make 8 kites from red fabric.

4. Sewing from point to point only and not into the seam allowances, sew a green B kite to a medium blue B kite. Press toward the green piece. Repeat to make 4. Again only sewing from point to point, sew a red C kite to each pair. Press toward the B kites.

5. Sewing from point to point only, sew a light beige A to each remaining red C kite. Sew a light beige A reverse to each unit. Press.

6. Sewing from point to point only, sew each unit created in Step 4 to a unit created in Step 5. Press toward the light beige A reverse piece.

7. Sewing from point to point only, sew the units created in Step 6 into pairs to make 2 block halves. Press.

8. Sewing from point to point only and in the order and direction shown, sew the block halves together. Press.

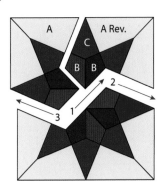

The template patterns are on page 119.

1. From light beige fabric, make 8 parallelograms using template A. Flip the template and make 8 A reverse.

2. From green fabric:

- Cut 4 squares 2″ × 2″ (B).

- Make 4 squares using template C.

- Cut 2 squares 2⅜″ × 2⅜″. Cut each square in half diagonally once to make 4 triangles (D).

3. Sewing only from point to point and not into the seam allowances, sew a light beige A to a light beige A reverse. Use Y-seam construction to sew a green C square to the unit. Press. Repeat to make 4.

4. Sewing from point to point only, sew a green B square to each unit from Step 3. Press.

5. Use Y-seam construction to sew the units created in Step 4 into pairs. Press. Sew the pairs together. Press.

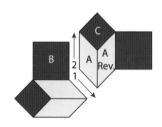

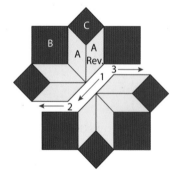

6. Use Y-seam construction to sew the remaining light beige A and A reverse pieces to the central star, sewing only from point to point and not into the seam allowances. Press.

7. Mark the center of each green D triangle and match it to the center of each A reverse/B/A unit. Sew the 4 green D triangles to the block. Press.

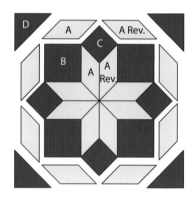

The template pattern is on page 120.

1. From light beige fabric, cut 4 squares 2⅛″ × 2⅛″. Cut each square in half diagonally once to make 8 triangles (A).

2. From light brown fabric, cut 4 rectangles 1½″ × 3″ (B).

3. From red fabric:

- Cut 1 square 1½″ × 1½″ (C).

- Make 4 parallelograms using template E. Flip the template and make 4 E reverse parallelograms.

4. From very light brown fabric, cut 4 squares 1¾″ × 1¾″ (D).

5. Sewing from point to point only, sew each red E to a red E reverse.

6. Use Y-seam construction to sew a very light brown D square to each E / reverse E pair. Press.

7. Sew 2 light beige A triangles to each unit created in Step 6. Press.

8. Sew 2 units created in Step 7 to opposite sides of a light brown B rectangle to make the top row. Press. Repeat to make the bottom row.

9. Sew 2 light brown B rectangles to opposite sides of the red C square to make the center row. Press.

10. Sew the 3 rows together. Press.

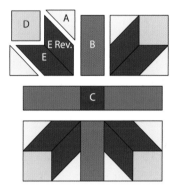

1. From light beige fabric:

- Cut 4 squares 2⅜″ × 2⅜″ (A). Cut 2 squares in half diagonally to make 4 triangles (B).

- Cut 1 square 4¼″ × 4¼″. Cut the square in half diagonally twice to make 4 triangles (C).

2. From medium blue fabric:

- Cut 2 squares 2⅜″ × 2⅜″ (A).

- Cut 1 square 4¼″ × 4¼″. Cut the square in half diagonally twice to make 4 triangles (C).

3. From red fabric, cut 2 squares 2⅜″ × 2⅜″. Cut each square in half diagonally once to make 4 triangles (B).

4. Refer to Quick-Pieced HST Units (page 14, Abel's Favorite, Step 3) to make 4 quick-pieced HST units with the medium blue and light beige A squares.

5. Sew a light beige B triangle to each HST unit. Press. Sew a red B triangle to each unit. Press.

6. Sew each medium blue C triangle to a light beige C triangle. Press.

7. Sew each unit created in Step 5 to a unit created in Step 6. Press.

8. Arrange the block segments as shown in the block assembly diagram. Sew into 2 rows. Press.

9. Sew the 2 rows together. Press.

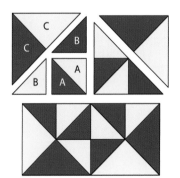

PENNSYLVANIA

1. From light beige fabric, cut 4 rectangles 1½″ × 2½″ (A) and 4 rectangles 1½″ × 4½″ (B).

2. From medium blue fabric, cut 1 square 2½″ × 2½″ (C) and 8 squares 1½″ × 1½″ (D).

3. Sew 2 light beige A rectangles to opposite sides of the medium blue C square to make the block center. Press.

4. Sew 2 medium blue D squares to opposite ends of the remaining light beige A rectangles. Press.

5. Sew the strips created in Step 4 to the top and bottom of the block center. Press.

6. Sew 2 light beige B rectangles to opposite sides of the block center. Press.

7. Sew 2 medium blue D squares to opposite ends of the remaining light beige B rectangles. Press.

8. Sew the strips created in Step 7 to the top and bottom of the block center. Press.

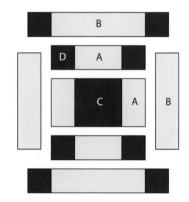

PETERSBURG

The template pattern is on page 119.

1. From light brown fabric:
- Cut 1 square 5¼″ × 5¼″ (A).
- Cut 1 square 1⅞″ × 1⅞″ (F).

2. From green fabric, cut 4 squares 1⅞″ × 1⅞″. Cut each square in half diagonally once to make 8 triangles (B).

3. From red fabric, make 4 pentagons using template C.

4. From light beige fabric:
- Cut 4 squares 2⅞″ × 2⅞″ (D).

- Cut 4 squares 1½″ × 1½″ (E).

5. Refer to Quick-Pieced Square-On-Point Unit (page 14, Abel's Favorite, Step 5) to make a quick-pieced square-on-point unit with 1 light brown A square and 4 light beige D squares. Then cut the square-on-point unit in half diagonally twice to create 4 side triangle units.

6. Sew a green B triangle to a light beige E square. Press toward the green fabric. Repeat to make 4.

7. Sew a green B triangle to a red C pentagon. Press toward the red fabric. Repeat to make 4.

8. Sew a unit created in Step 6 to a unit created in Step 7. Press. Repeat to make 4.

9. Sew 2 of the units created in Step 8 to opposite sides of the light brown F square to make the center row. Press.

10. Sew 2 of the side triangle units created in Step 5 to opposite sides of a unit created in Step 8. Press. Repeat to make a second row.

11. Arrange the block segments into 3 diagonal rows as shown in the block assembly diagram. Sew the rows together. Press.

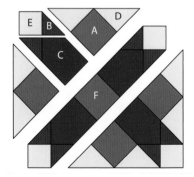

1. From light beige fabric:

- Cut 4 squares 2″ × 2″ (A).

- Cut 1 square 4¼″ × 4¼″ (B).

- Cut 2 squares 2⅜″ × 2⅜″. Cut each square in half diagonally once to make 4 triangles (C).

- Cut 1 square 2¾″ × 2¾″. Cut the square in half diagonally twice to make 4 triangles (D).

2. From red fabric:

- Cut 4 squares 2⅜″ × 2⅜″ (C).

- Cut 1 square 2¾″ × 2¾″. Cut the square in half diagonally twice to make 4 triangles (D).

3. Refer to Quick-Pieced Flying Geese Units (page 14, Abel's Favorite, Step 4) to make 4 quick-pieced Flying Geese units with 4 red C squares and 1 light beige B square.

4. Sew 2 light beige A squares to opposite sides of a Flying Geese unit as shown to make the top row. Press. Repeat to make the bottom row.

5. Sew each light beige D triangle to a red D triangle. Press. Sew a light beige C triangle to each unit. Press.

6. Sew the units created in Step 5 together in pairs. Press. Sew the pairs together to make the central Pinwheel. Press.

7. Sew 2 Flying Geese units to opposite sides of the central Pinwheel to make the center row. Press.

8. Sew the 3 rows together. Press.

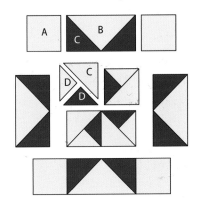

1. From light beige fabric:

- Cut 2 squares 2⅜″ × 2⅜″ (A).

- Cut 1 square 5⅜″ × 5⅜″. Cut the square in half diagonally once to make 2 triangles (C). From a C triangle, cut a square 2⅜″ × 2⅜″ and cut in half diagonally once to make 2 triangles (B). From the remaining scrap, cut another B triangle for a total of 3.

2. From dark blue fabric:

- Cut 2 squares 2⅜″ × 2⅜″ (A).

- Cut 1 square 5⅜″ × 5⅜″. Cut the square in half diagonally once to make 2 triangles (C). From a C triangle, cut a square 2⅜″ × 2⅜″ and cut in half diagonally once to make 2 triangles (B). From the remaining scrap, cut another B triangle for a total of 3.

3. Refer to Quick-Pieced HST Units (page 14, Abel's Favorite, Step 3) to make 4 quick-pieced HST units with the dark blue and light beige A squares.

4. Sew a light beige B triangle to an HST unit. Press. Repeat to make 3.

5. Sew a dark blue B triangle to 2 of the units created in Step 4. Press.

6. Sew the remaining dark blue B triangle to the remaining HST unit. Press.

7. Arrange the HST units into 4 offset rows as shown in the block assembly diagram. Sew the rows together, pressing after each addition.

8. Following the block assembly diagram, sew the dark blue C triangle to the unit created in Step 7. Press. Sew the light beige C triangle to the opposite side. Press.

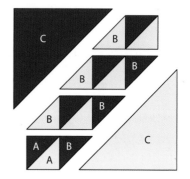

The template patterns are on page 120.

1. From green fabric:

- Make 4 rectangles using template A.

- Make 16 triangles using template B.

- Cut 2 squares 2⅞″ × 2⅞″. Cut each square in half once diagonally to make 4 triangles (D). Mark ¼″ seam allowances on the back of each if desired.

2. From light brown fabric, make 4 rhombuses using template C. Flip the template and make 4 C reverses.

3. From light beige fabric:

- Make 4 trapezoids using template E.

- Make 4 trapezoids using template F.

- Make 1 octagon using template G.

4. Sew 4 green B triangles to opposite long sides of the light beige G octagon to make the block center. Press.

5. Sew a green B triangle to one short side of each C rhombus and each C reverse. Press.

6. Sewing only from point to point, sew 1 C unit and 1 C reverse unit to opposite sides of a green A rectangle. Press. Use Y-seam construction to sew a light beige E trapezoid between the star points. Press. Repeat this step to make 4 identical units.

7. Sew a green D triangle and a green B triangle to each light beige F trapezoid. Press. Repeat to make 4 block corners.

8. Following the block assembly diagram, sew the units into 3 rows. Press. Sew the 3 rows together. Press.

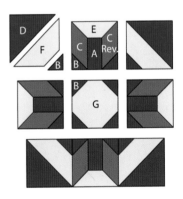

RAILROAD CROSSING

The template pattern is on page 120.

1. From light beige fabric:

- Cut 2 squares 2½″ × 2½″. Cut each square in half diagonally once to make 4 triangles (A).

- Cut 1 square 4¼″ × 4¼″. Cut the square in half diagonally twice to make 4 triangles (B).

2. From red fabric, make 8 rectangles using template D.

3. From dark brown fabric:

- Cut 1 square 2⅝″ × 2⅝″ (C).

- Make 4 rectangles using template D.

4. Sew 2 red D rectangles to opposite sides of each dark brown D rectangle. Repeat to make 4 D units. Press.

5. Sew 2 units created in Step 4 to opposite sides of the dark brown C square. Press.

6. Sew 2 light beige A triangles to opposite sides of the unit made in Step 5 to make the center row. Press.

7. Sew 2 light beige B triangles to opposite sides of a unit created in Step 4. Press. Sew a light beige A triangle to the top to make the top row. Press. Repeat this step to make the bottom row.

8. Sew the 3 rows together. Press. Trim the block to 6½″ × 6½″ unfinished.

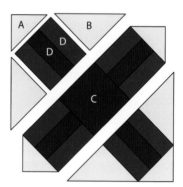

RESOLUTION SQUARE

1. From light beige fabric, cut 2 squares 2″ × 2″ (A) and 2 rectangles 2″ × 3½″ (B).

2. From dark brown fabric, cut 2 squares 2″ × 2″ (A).

3. From light brown fabric, cut 2 squares 3½″ × 3½″ (C).

4. Sew each light beige A square to a dark brown A square. Press.

5. Sew a light beige B rectangle to each square pair. Press.

6. Sew a light brown C square to each unit to make 2 rows. Press.

7. Sew the rows together. Press.

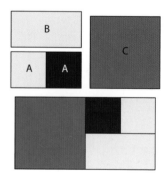

The template patterns are on pages 106 and 120.

1. From medium blue fabric:

- Make 1 square using template A.

- Cut 2 squares 3¼″ × 3¼″. Cut each square in half diagonally twice to make 8 triangles (B).

2. From light beige fabric:

- Cut 2 squares 1⅞″ × 1⅞″. Cut each square in half diagonally once to make 4 triangles (C).

- Make 4 squares using template D.

- Cut 1 square 3¼″ × 3¼″. Cut the square in half diagonally twice to make 4 triangles (B).

- Cut 4 squares 2½″ × 2½″ (E).

3. From red fabric, cut 2 squares 2¼″ × 2¼″. Cut each square in half diagonally twice to make 8 triangles (F).

4. Sew 2 red F triangles to each light beige C triangle to make 4 Flying Geese units. Press.

5. Sew 2 Flying Geese units to opposite sides of the medium blue A square as shown. Press.

6. Sew 2 light beige D squares to opposite ends of the remaining Flying Geese units. Press.

7. Sew the rows made in Step 6 to opposite sides of the row made in Step 5 to make the central star. Press.

8. Sew 2 medium blue B triangles to adjacent sides of each light beige E square to make 4 block corners. Press.

9. Sew 2 block corners to opposite sides of the central star. Press.

10. Sew 2 light beige B triangles to opposite sides of the remaining block corners. Press. Sew the units to the remaining sides of the central star. Press.

The template pattern is on page 120.

1. From light beige fabric:

- Cut 2 squares 2⅞″ × 2⅞″ (A).

- Cut 8 squares 1⅞″ × 1⅞″. Cut each square in half diagonally once to make 16 triangles (B).

2. From red fabric:

- Cut 2 squares 2⅞″ × 2⅞″ (A).

- Cut 1 square 2½″ × 2½″ (C).

- Make 8 squares using template D.

3. From dark brown fabric, make 8 squares using template D.

4. Sew each dark brown D square to a red D square. Press. Sew the units together in pairs to make 4 Four-Patches. Press.

5. Sew 2 light beige B triangles to opposite sides of a Four-Patch. Press. Sew 2 light beige B triangles to the other 2 sides of the same Four-Patch. Press. Repeat this step for each Four-Patch.

6. Refer to Quick-Pieced HST Units (page 14, Abel's Favorite, Step 3) to make 4 quick-pieced HST units with the red and light beige A squares.

7. Sew 2 HST units to opposite sides of a unit created in Step 5 to make the top row. Press. Repeat to make the bottom row.

8. Sew the remaining 2 units created in Step 5 to opposite sides of the red C square to make the center row. Press.

9. Sew the 3 rows together. Press.

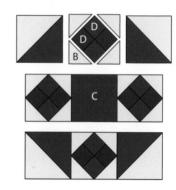

The template pattern is on page 121.

1. From light beige fabric, cut 4 squares 2⅜″ × 2⅜″ (A).

2. From light beige fabric, cut 1 square 3½″ × 3½″ (C). Fold in half vertically, horizontally, and diagonally to mark the appliqué placement lines.

3. From red fabric, cut 1 square 4¼″ × 4¼″ (B).

4. From medium blue fabric, cut 4 squares 2″ × 2″ (D).

5. From medium blue fabric, make 4 of appliqué template E. *Note:* It is not necessary to add a seam allowance to the straight edges of the template. To the curve, add the seam allowance required by your preferred appliqué method.

6. Place a medium blue E appliqué motif on the light beige C square. With right sides up and straight edges aligned, appliqué the curve in place using your preferred method. Appliqué another E piece to the opposite side of the square and then to the other 2 sides. *Note:* It is not necessary to appliqué the straight edges as they will be covered by other seams.

7. Refer to Quick-Pieced Flying Geese Units (page 14, Abel's Favorite, Step 4) to make 4 quick-pieced Flying Geese units with the light beige A squares and the red B square.

8. Sew 2 Flying Geese units to opposite sides of the appliqué square to make the center row. Press.

9. Sew 2 medium blue D squares to opposite sides of each remaining Flying Geese unit to make the top and bottom rows. Press.

10. Sew the rows together. Press.

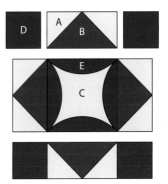

The template patterns are on pages 120 and 121.

1. From green fabric:

- Make 4 triangles using template A.

- Cut 2 squares 2⅜″ × 2⅜″ (B).

2. From medium blue fabric:

- Cut 1 square 2″ × 2″ (C).

- Cut 2 squares 2⅜″ × 2⅜″ (B).

3. From light beige fabric:

- Cut 4 squares 2⅜″ × 2⅜″. Cut each square in half diagonally once to make 8 triangles (B).

- Make 4 triangles using template D.

4. Refer to Quick-Pieced HST Units (page 14, Abel's Favorite, Step 3) to make 4 quick-pieced HST units with the green and medium blue B squares.

5. Sew 2 light beige B triangles to adjacent sides of each HST unit to make 4 block corners. Press.

6. Sewing from point to point only, sew 2 light beige D triangles to opposite sides of the green C square. Press. Sew the other light beige D triangles to the other 2 sides, sewing only from point to point. Press.

7. Use Y-seam construction to sew 2 green A triangles to opposite sides of the unit created in Step 6. Press. Sew on the remaining 2 green A triangles to complete the block center. Press.

8. Sew 2 block corners to opposite sides of the block center. Press. Sew on the remaining 2 block corners. Press.

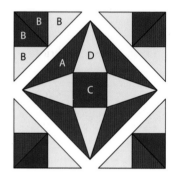

The template patterns are on page 120.

1. From light beige fabric, cut 4 squares 4″ × 4″ (A).

2. From dark brown fabric, make 4 of template B, adding the appropriate seam allowance for your preferred appliqué method.

3. From very light brown fabric, cut 4 D elliptical shapes at least ⅛″ bigger all around than the cutout center of the B appliqué template but smaller than the outer edge of the B template.

4. From dark brown fabric, cut 8 squares 1¼″ × 1¼″ (C). Mark a diagonal line on the back of each C square.

5. Align a very light brown B piece along the diagonal of a light beige A square. Baste or pin in place.

6. Using your preferred method, reverse appliqué the inner edge of a dark brown B piece to the very light brown D piece, sewing through the dark brown B, the very light brown D, and the light beige A pieces. Appliqué the outer edge of the dark brown B piece to the light beige A square.

7. Keeping the appliquéd pieces centered, trim the light beige A square to 3½″ × 3½″.

8. Place a dark brown C square in one corner of the light beige A square over one end of the appliquéd motif, right sides facing and edges aligned with the light beige square. Sew a diagonal seam along the drawn line from corner to corner of the dark brown C square and from edge to edge of the light beige A square. Trim the excess fabric

¼″ from the seam. Press open. Repeat this step with another C square in the opposite corner.

9. Repeat Step 8 to make 4 identical units.

10. Sew the units together in mirror-image pairs to make 2 rows. Press. Sew the rows together.

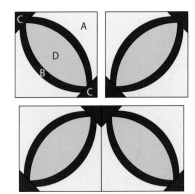

SPOTSYLVANIA COURT HOUSE

The foundation pattern is on page 121.

1. Complete a foundation paper piecing pattern for the block center using green, light brown, and light beige fabrics as indicated.

2. Cut 6 squares 1⅞″ × 1⅞″ (A) from light beige fabric and 6 squares 1⅞″ × 1⅞″ (A) from green.

3. Refer to Quick-Pieced HST Units (page 14, Abel's Favorite, Step 3) to make 12 quick-pieced HST units with green and light beige A squares.

4. From light beige fabric, cut 4 rectangles 1½″ × 2½″ (B).

5. Sew an HST unit to opposite ends of each light beige B rectangle. Press.

6. Sew 2 of the units from Step 5 to opposite sides of the block center to make the middle row. Press.

7. Add an HST unit to opposite ends of the remaining units from Step 5 to make the top and bottom rows. Press.

8. Sew the 3 rows together. Press.

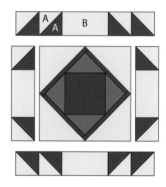

SPURS

1. From light beige fabric, cut 2 squares 2⅜″ × 2⅜″ (A) and 8 squares 2″ × 2″ (B).

2. From light brown fabric, cut 2 squares 2⅜″ × 2⅜″ (A).

3. From red fabric, cut 4 rectangles 2″ × 3½″ (C).

4. Draw a solid diagonal line from corner to corner on the wrong side of a B square. Place a B square

on a red C rectangle, right sides facing and edges aligned, with the drawn line oriented as shown. Sew on the drawn line. Trim the excess fabric ¼″ away from the seam. Press toward the light beige fabric. Repeat to make 4 B/C units.

5. Refer to Quick-Pieced HST Units (page 14, Abel's Favorite, Step 3) to make 4 quick-pieced HST units with light beige and light brown A squares.

6. Sew each HST unit to a light beige B square. Press.

7. Sew each unit created in Step 6 to a B/C unit to make 4 block quarters. Press.

8. Following the block assembly diagram, sew the block quarters into pairs to make 2 rows. Press.

9. Sew the rows together. Press.

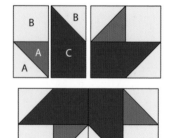

The foundation patterns are on page 122.

1. Make 4 of foundation paper piecing pattern A using light beige and medium blue fabrics. Press.

2. Make 4 of foundation paper piecing pattern B using red and light beige fabrics. Press.

3. Make 1 of foundation paper piecing pattern C using red, light beige, and medium blue fabrics. Press.

4. Sew 2 foundation paper piecing A units to opposite sides of a foundation paper piecing B unit to make the top row. Press. Repeat to make the bottom row.

5. Sew 2 foundation paper piecing B units to opposite sides of the foundation paper piecing C unit to make the center row. Press.

6. Sew the 3 rows together. Press.

1. From light beige fabric:

- Cut 4 squares 2½″ × 2½″ (A).
- Cut 4 squares 1½″ × 1½″ (B).
- Cut 2 squares 2⅞″ × 2⅞″. Cut each square in half diagonally once to make 4 triangles (C).

2. From red fabric:

- Cut 4 squares 1⅞″ × 1⅞″. Cut each square in half diagonally once to make 8 triangles (D).
- Cut 1 square 2½″ × 2½″ (E).

- Cut 8 squares 1½″ × 1½″ (F). Draw a diagonal line from corner to corner on the back of each F square.

3. Sew 2 red D triangles to adjacent sides of each light beige B square. Press. Sew a light beige C triangle to each unit. Press.

4. Aligning the corners, sew on the drawn line, press, and trim an F square on one corner of the A square and then sew another F square to an adjacent corner. Repeat this step to make a total of 4 A/F units.

5. Sew 2 units created in Step 4 to opposite sides of the red F square to make the center row. Press.

6. Sew 2 units created in Step 3 to opposite sides of a unit created in Step 4 to make the top row. Press. Repeat to make the bottom row.

7. Sew the 3 rows together. Press.

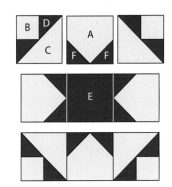

The foundation patterns are on page 121.

1. Make 4 of foundation paper piecing pattern A using light beige and dark brown fabrics. Press.

2. Make 4 of foundation paper piecing pattern B using medium blue and light beige fabrics. Press.

3. Make 1 of foundation paper piecing pattern C using medium blue and light beige fabrics. Press.

4. Sew 2 foundation paper piecing A units to opposite sides of a foundation paper piecing B unit to make the top row. Press. Repeat to make the bottom row.

5. Sew 2 foundation paper piecing B units to opposite sides of the foundation paper piecing C unit to make the center row. Press.

6. Sew the 3 rows together. Press.

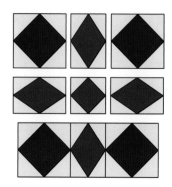

The template pattern is on page 122.

1. From light beige fabric, cut 1 square 6½″ × 6½″. Fold the square in half horizontally, vertically, and twice diagonally, pressing each fold to mark the appliqué placement lines. *Note:* You can also cut the square larger and trim to size after sewing the appliqués in place, if desired.

2. From green fabric, make 12 of the tea leaf template A, adding the required seam allowance for your preferred appliqué method.

3. Following the appliqué placement diagram (page 123) and working from the center outward, appliqué the 12 green A pieces in place.

1. From light beige fabric:

- Cut 8 squares 1⅞″ × 1⅞″ (A).

- Cut 6 squares 1½″ × 1½″ (B).

- Cut 2 rectangles 1½″ × 2½″ (C).

2. From red fabric:

- Cut 8 squares 1⅞″ × 1⅞″ (A).

- Cut 6 squares 1½″ × 1½″ (B).

- Cut 2 rectangles 1½″ × 2½″ (C).

3. Refer to Quick-Pieced HST Units (page 14, Abel's Favorite, Step 3) to make 16 quick-pieced HST units with the 8 red A squares and 8 light beige A squares.

Following the block assembly diagram for correct placement, complete the following steps:

4. Sew the HST units together to make 4 pairs and 4 mirror-image pairs. Press.

5. Sew a light beige B square to a red B square. Press. Repeat to make 4 pairs. Sew a light beige or red C rectangle to each pair as shown. Press.

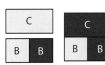

6. Sew a paired HST unit to each unit created in Step 5. Press.

7. Sew either a light beige B square or a red B square to the end of each remaining paired HST unit. Press.

8. Sew each unit created in Step 7 to a unit created in Step 6 to make 4 block quarters. Press.

9. Sew the block quarters into 2 rows. Press. Sew the rows together. Press.

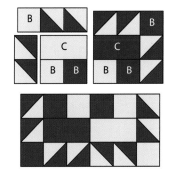

1. From light beige fabric:

- Cut 1 strip 1½″ × 14″.

- Cut 8 squares 1⅞″ × 1⅞″ (A).

2. From medium blue fabric:

- Cut 2 squares 3¼″ × 3¼″ (B).

- Cut 1 square 2½″ × 2½″ (C).

3. From dark brown fabric, cut 1 strip 1½″ × 14″.

4. Sew the dark brown strip and the light beige strip together along the longest side. Press toward the dark brown fabric. Use a rotary cutter to crosscut 8 strips 1½″ wide.

5. Rotate 1 crosscut strip 180° and sew it to another. Repeat to make 4 Four-Patches. Press.

6. Refer to Quick-Pieced Flying Geese Units (page 14, Abel's Favorite, Step 4) to make 8 quick-pieced Flying Geese units with the 8 light beige A squares and the 2 medium blue B squares.

7. Sew the Flying Geese units together in pairs. Press.

8. Arrange the block segments as shown in the block assembly diagram and sew into 3 rows. Press.

9. Sew the 3 rows together. Press.

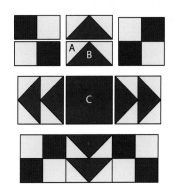

1. From light beige fabric:

- Cut 4 squares 2½″ × 2½″ (A).

- Cut 1 square 3¼″ × 3¼″. Cut the square in half diagonally twice to make 4 light beige triangles (B).

2. From red fabric, cut 2 squares 2⅞″ × 2⅞″. Cut each square in half diagonally once to make 4 red triangles (C).

3. From dark brown fabric:

- Cut 1 square 2½″ × 2½″ (A).

- Cut 1 square 3¼″ × 3¼″. Cut the square in half diagonally twice to make 4 dark brown triangles (B).

Following the block assembly diagram for correct placement, complete the following steps:

4. Pair each dark brown B triangle with a light beige B triangle and sew along a short side to make 4 identical dark star points. Press.

5. Sew each B/B triangle pair to a red C triangle. Press.

6. Arrange the block pieces into 3 rows. Sew the 3 rows together. Press.

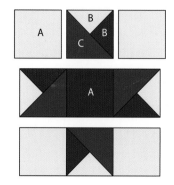

1. From light beige fabric:

- Cut 4 squares 1⅞″ × 1⅞″ (A).

- Cut 2 squares 1½″ × 1½″ (B).

- Cut 2 squares 3½″ × 3½″ (C).

2. From medium brown fabric:

- Cut 4 squares 1⅞″ × 1⅞″ (A).

- Cut 2 squares 2½″ × 2½″ (D).

3. Refer to Quick-Pieced HST Units (page 14, Abel's Favorite, Step 3) to make 8 quick-pieced HST units with the medium brown and the light beige A squares.

Following the block assembly diagram for correct placement, complete the following steps:

4. Sew the HST units together to make 2 pairs and 2 mirror-image pairs. Press.

5. Sew a paired HST unit to each medium brown D square. Press.

6. Sew a light beige B square to each mirror-image paired HST unit. Press.

7. Sew a unit created in Step 5 to each unit created in Step 6. Press.

8. Sew each unit created in Step 7 to a light beige C square to make a row. Press.

9. Sew the 2 rows together. Press.

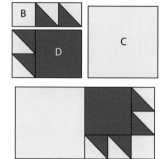

Traditional Piecing

1. From light beige fabric:

- Cut 8 squares 1⅞″ × 1⅞″ (A).

- Cut 4 squares 1½″ × 1½″ (B).

- Cut 1 square 3¼″ × 3¼″. Cut the square in half diagonally twice to make 4 triangles (C).

2. From red fabric:

- Cut 4 squares 1⅞″ × 1⅞″ (A).

- Cut 2 squares 2⅞″ × 2⅞″. Cut each square in half diagonally once to make 4 triangles (D).

3. From light brown fabric:

- Cut 4 squares 1⅞″ × 1⅞″ (A).

- Cut 1 square 2½″ × 2½″ (E).

4. Refer to Quick-Pieced HST Units (page 14, Abel's Favorite, Step 3) to make 8 quick-pieced HST units with the 4 red A squares and 4 of the light beige A squares.

5. Repeat Step 4 with the light brown A squares and the remaining light beige A squares to make 8 light brown and light beige HST units.

Follow the block assembly diagram for correct placement as you complete the following steps:

6. Sew each red / light beige HST unit to a light brown / light beige HST unit to make 4 pairs and 4 mirror-image pairs. Press.

7. Sew each paired HST unit to a mirror-image paired HST unit. Press.

8. Sew 2 light beige C triangles to opposite sides of the light brown E square. Press. Sew 2 light beige C triangles to the remaining two sides. Press.

9. Sew 2 red D triangles to opposite sides of the unit created in Step 8. Press. Sew 2 red D triangles to the remaining two sides. Press.

10. Sew 2 units created in Step 7 to opposite sides of the unit created in Step 9 to make the center row. Press.

11. Sew 2 light beige B squares to opposite ends of the remaining units from Step 7 to make the top and bottom rows. Press.

12. Sew the 3 rows together. Press.

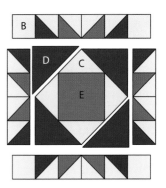

Foundation Paper Piecing

The foundation patterns are on pages 123 and 124.

1. Make 1 of foundation paper piecing pattern A using light brown, light beige, and red fabrics. Press.

2. Make 2 of foundation paper piecing pattern B using light brown, light beige, and red fabrics. Press.

3. Make 2 of foundation paper piecing pattern C using light brown, light beige, and red fabrics. Press.

4. Sew the 2 foundation paper piecing B units to opposite sides of the foundation paper piecing A unit to make the center row. Press.

5. Sew a foundation paper piecing C unit to the top and bottom of the center row. Press.

Traditional Piecing

The template pattern is on page 124.

1. From medium blue fabric, cut 1 square 2″ × 2″ (A).

2. From light beige fabric:

- Cut 8 squares 1⅝″ × 1⅝″. Cut each square in half diagonally once to make 16 triangles (D).

- Cut 2 squares 2⅜″ × 2⅜″. Cut each square in half diagonally once to make 4 triangles (E).

- Cut 4 rectangles 1¼″ × 3½″ (F).

3. From dark brown fabric:

- Cut 1 square 2¾″ × 2¾″. Cut the square in half diagonally twice to make 4 triangles (B).

- Make 4 squares using template C.

- Cut 4 rectangles 1¼″ × 3½″ (F).

4. Sew 2 light beige D triangles to opposite sides of a dark brown C square. Press. Sew 2 light beige D triangles to the other 2 sides. Press. Repeat with remaining D triangles and C squares to make 4 corner units.

5. Sew each light beige F rectangle to a dark brown F rectangle along the long edges. Press.

6. Sew 2 dark brown B triangles to opposite sides of the medium blue A square. Press. Sew 2 dark brown B triangles to the other 2 sides. Sew 2 light beige E triangles to opposite sides of the unit. Sew 2 light beige E triangles to the other 2 sides. Press.

7. Following the block assembly diagram, sew the units into 3 rows. Press.

8. Sew the 3 rows together. Press.

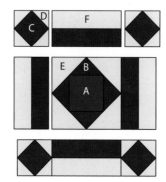

Foundation Paper Piecing

The foundation patterns are on pages 124 and 125.

1. Make 1 of foundation paper piecing pattern A using medium blue, dark brown, and light beige fabrics. Press.

2. Make 4 of foundation paper piecing pattern B using light beige and dark brown fabrics. Press.

3. Cut 2 rectangles 1¼″ × 3½″ from light beige fabric and 2 from dark brown. Sew each light beige rectangle to a dark brown rectangle along the long edges. Press.

4. Sew 2 foundation paper piecing B units to opposite sides of the rectangle pairs to make the top and bottom rows. Press.

5. Refer to the block assembly diagram (at left) to sew the top and bottom rows to the foundation paper piecing A unit. Press.

The template patterns are on pages 106 and 124.

1. Using template A, make 5 squares from light beige fabric and 4 from medium blue fabric.

2. From light brown fabric, make 4 pentagons using template B.

3. From medium blue fabric, cut 4 squares 1⅞″ × 1⅞″. Cut each square in half diagonally to make 8 triangles (C).

4. Sew 2 light beige A squares to opposite sides of a medium blue A square. Press. Repeat to make a second identical row. Sew 2 medium blue A squares to opposite sides of a light beige A square. Press. Sew the 3 rows together to make the central Nine-Patch. Press.

5. Sew 2 medium blue C triangles to each light brown B pentagon as shown in the block assembly

diagram to make 4 block corners. Press.

6. Sew 2 block corners to opposite sides of the central Nine-Patch. Press. Sew on the other 2 block corners. Press.

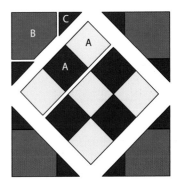

1. From light beige fabric:

■ Cut 2 squares 2⅜″ × 2⅜″ (A).

■ Cut 1 square 4¼″ × 4¼″ (B).

2. From very light brown fabric, cut 2 squares 2⅜″ × 2⅜″ (A).

3. From red fabric, cut 8 squares 2⅜″ × 2⅜″ (A).

4. Refer to Quick-Pieced Flying Geese Units (page 14, Abel's Favorite, Step 4) to make

4 quick-pieced Flying Geese units with 4 of the red A squares and the light beige B square.

5. Refer to Quick-Pieced HST Units (page 14, Abel's Favorite, Step 3) to make 4 quick-pieced HST units with 2 red A squares and 2 light beige A squares.

6. Repeat Step 5 using the very light brown A squares and the remaining red A squares to make 4 red/very light brown HST units.

7. Sew 2 red/very light brown HST units together as shown in the block assembly diagram. Press toward the red fabric. Repeat to make a second, identical unit. Sew the 2 units together to make the central Pinwheel. Press.

8. Sew 2 Flying Geese units to opposite sides of the central Pinwheel to make the center row. Press.

9. Sew 2 red/light beige HST units to opposite sides of the remaining Flying Geese units as shown to make the top and bottom rows. Press.

10. Sew the 3 rows together. Press.

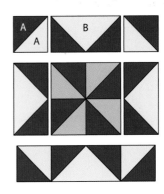

The template patterns are on pages 124 and 125.

1. From medium blue fabric:

- Cut 2 squares 2⅝" × 2⅝". Cut each square in half diagonally once to make 4 triangles (A).

- Make 4 triangles using template C. Flip the template and make 4 C reverse.

2. From light beige fabric:

- Make 4 triangles using template B.

- Make 4 kites using template D.

- Make 4 triangles using template E.

3. From light brown fabric, make 12 triangles using template B.

4. Sew a medium blue C triangle to each light beige D kite. Press. Sew a medium blue C reverse triangle to each light beige E triangle. Press. Sew each C/D unit to a C reverse / E unit. Press.

5. Sew 3 light brown B triangles to each light beige B triangle. Press. Sew a medium blue A triangle to each unit. Press.

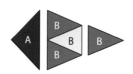

6. Sew each unit created in Step 4 to a unit created in Step 5 as shown in the block assembly diagram to make a block quarter. Press.

7. Sew the block quarters together in pairs. Press.

8. Sew the pairs together. Press.

Note: If you prefer foundation paper piecing, make 1 of foundation paper piecing pattern A from Union (Block J-8, page 124) rather than following Steps 5 and 6 (at right). Cut your pieces for the C, D, and E sections slightly larger than the sizes provided below.

1. From light beige fabric:

- Cut 6 squares $1\frac{7}{8}'' \times 1\frac{7}{8}''$ (A).

- Cut 4 rectangles $1\frac{1}{2}'' \times 2\frac{1}{2}''$ (B).

- Cut 1 square $3\frac{1}{4}'' \times 3\frac{1}{4}''$. Cut the square in half diagonally twice to make 4 triangles (C).

2. From green fabric, cut 2 squares $2\frac{7}{8}'' \times 2\frac{7}{8}''$. Cut each square in half diagonally once to make 4 triangles (D).

3. From red fabric, cut 6 squares $1\frac{7}{8}'' \times 1\frac{7}{8}''$ (A) and 1 square $2\frac{1}{2}'' \times 2\frac{1}{2}''$ (E).

4. Refer to Quick-Pieced HST Units (page 14, Abel's Favorite, Step 3) to make 12 quick-pieced HST units with the 6 red and 6 light beige A squares.

5. Sew 2 light beige C triangles to opposite sides of the red E square. Press. Sew the remaining light beige C triangles to the other 2 sides. Press.

6. Sew 2 green D triangles to opposite sides of the unit created in Step 5. Press. Sew the remaining green D triangles to the other 2 sides to complete the block center. Press.

7. Sew 2 HST units to opposite ends of each light beige B rectangle, referring to the block assembly diagram for placement. Press.

8. Sew 2 of the strips created in Step 7 to opposite sides of the block center to make the middle row. Press.

9. Sew an HST unit to each end of the remaining strips to make the top and bottom rows. Press.

10. Sew the 3 rows together. Press.

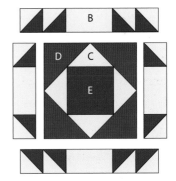

Traditional Piecing

The template pattern is on page 126.

1. From light beige fabric:

- Make 4 parallelograms using template A. Flip the template and make 4 A reverse.

- Cut 1 square 2¾″ × 2¾″. Cut the square in half diagonally twice to make 4 triangles (B).

2. From green fabric, cut 6 squares 2⅜″ × 2⅜″. Cut each square in half diagonally once to make 12 triangles (C).

3. From light brown fabric, cut 1 square 4¼″ × 4¼″. Cut the square in half diagonally twice to make 4 triangles (D).

4. From dark brown fabric, cut 1 square 2″ × 2″ (E).

5. Sew 2 light beige B triangles to opposite sides of the dark brown E square. Press. Sew the remaining light beige B triangles to the other 2 sides. Press.

6. Sew 2 green C triangles to opposite sides of the unit created in Step 5. Press. Sew the remaining green triangles to the other 2 sides. Press.

7. Sew 2 light brown D triangles to opposite sides of the unit created in Step 6. Press. Sew the remaining light brown D triangles to the other 2 sides to make the block center. Press.

8. Sew 1 A and 1 A reverse to a green C triangle as shown in the block assembly diagram. Press. Make 4.

9. Sew another green C triangle to each unit created in Step 8 to make 4 block corners. Press.

10. Sew 2 block corners to opposite sides of the block center. Press. Sew the remaining block corners to the other 2 sides. Press.

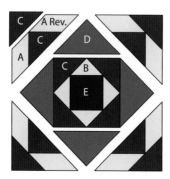

Foundation Paper Piecing

The foundation patterns are on pages 125 and 126.

1. Make 1 of foundation paper piecing pattern A using dark brown, light brown, green, and light beige fabrics to make the block center. Press.

2. Make 4 of foundation paper piecing pattern B using light beige and green fabrics to make 4 block corners. Press.

3. Sew 2 block corners to opposite sides of the block center. Press.

4. Sew the remaining block corners to the other 2 sides of the block center. Press.

Traditional Piecing

1. From light beige fabric:

- Cut 6 squares 2⅜″ × 2⅜″ (A).

- Cut 1 square 3½″ × 3½″ (D).

2. From red fabric, cut 1 square 4¼″ × 4¼″ (B).

3. From medium blue fabric:

- Cut 2 squares 2⅜″ × 2⅜″ (A).

- Cut 4 squares 2″ × 2″ (C).

4. Refer to Quick-Pieced Flying Geese Units (page 14, Abel's Favorite, Step 4) to make 4 quick-pieced Flying Geese units with 4 of the light beige A squares and the red B square.

5. Refer to Quick-Pieced Square-On-Point Unit (page 14, Abel's Favorite, Step 5) to make 1 quick-pieced square-on-point unit with the 4 medium blue C squares and the light beige D square.

6. Refer to Quick-Pieced HST Units (page 14, Abel's Favorite, Step 3) to make 4 quick-pieced HST units with the 2 medium blue A squares and the remaining light beige A squares.

7. Sew 2 Flying Geese units to opposite sides of the square-on-point unit as shown to make the center row. Press.

8. Sew 2 HST units to opposite sides of each remaining Flying Geese unit to make the top and bottom rows. Press.

9. Sew the rows together. Press.

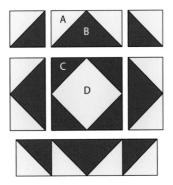

Foundation Paper Piecing

The foundation patterns are on pages 124 and 126.

1. Make 1 of foundation paper piecing pattern A using light beige, medium blue, and red fabrics. Press.

2. Make 2 of foundation paper piecing pattern B using light beige, medium blue, and red fabrics. Press.

3. Sew the 2 foundation paper piecing B units to the top and bottom of the A unit. Press.

The template patterns are on page 126.

1. From light beige fabric:

- Make 8 trapezoids using template A.

- Cut 2 squares 2½″ × 2½″. Cut each square in half diagonally twice to make 8 triangles (B).

2. Using template C, make 12 rhombuses from red fabric and 12 rhombuses from dark brown fabric.

3. From light brown fabric, cut 4 squares 2⅝″ × 2⅝″. Cut each square in half diagonally once to make 8 triangles (D).

Following the block assembly diagram for correct placement, complete the following steps:

4. Sew a red C rhombus and a dark brown C rhombus to each light beige B triangle as shown in the block assembly diagram. Press.

5. Sewing from point to point only, sew a unit created in Step 4 to a light brown D triangle. Use Y-seam construction to sew another unit to an adjacent side. Press. Repeat this step to make 4 identical units.

6. Sew each remaining dark brown C rhombus to a light beige A trapezoid. Press. Sew each remaining red C rhombus to a light beige A trapezoid. Press.

7. Sewing from point to point only, sew a dark brown C/A unit to a light brown D triangle. Use Y-seam construction to sew a red C/A unit to an adjacent side. Press. Repeat to make 4 units.

8. Sew each unit created in Step 5 to a unit created in Step 7 to make 4 block quarters. Press.

9. Sew the block quarters into pairs to make 2 rows as shown. Press.

10. Sew the 2 rows together. Press.

WINDMILL

1. From dark blue fabric, cut 2 squares 3⅞″ × 3⅞″. Cut each square in half diagonally once to make 4 triangles (A).

2. From red fabric, cut 1 square 4¼″ × 4¼″. Cut the square in half diagonally twice to make 4 triangles (B).

3. From light beige fabric, cut 1 square 4¼″ × 4¼″. Cut the square in half diagonally twice to make 4 triangles (B).

Following the block assembly diagram for correct placement, complete the following steps:

4. Sew each light beige B triangle to a red B triangle. Press.

5. Sew a dark blue A triangle to each B/B triangle pair to make 4 block quarters. Press.

6. Sew the block quarters into 2 rows as shown. Press.

7. Sew the rows together. Press.

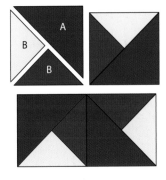

WINGED SQUARE

1. From light beige fabric:

- Cut 5 squares 2⅜″ × 2⅜″ (A).
- Cut 2 squares 2″ × 2″ (B).

2. From medium blue fabric:

- Cut 5 squares 2⅜″ × 2⅜″ (A).
- Cut 1 square 3½″ × 3½″ (C).

3. Refer to Quick-Pieced HST Units (page 14, Abel's Favorite, Step 3) to make 10 quick-pieced HST units with the 5 medium blue and 5 light beige A squares.

4. Sew 2 HST units together as shown in the block assembly diagram. Press. Repeat to make a second pair.

5. Sew the pairs from Step 4 to opposite sides of the medium blue C square to make the middle row. Press.

6. Sew 3 HST units together. Sew a light beige B square to the end to make the top row. Press. Repeat to make the bottom row.

7. Sew the 3 rows together. Press.

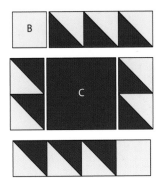

The template patterns are on pages 122 and 126.

1. From light beige fabric:

- Cut 6 squares 1⅞" × 1⅞". Cut each square in half diagonally once to make 12 triangles (A).

- Make 4 triangles using template B. Draw double hash marks for matching on the seam allowances as noted on the template.

2. From light brown fabric:

- Cut 1 square 2¾" × 2¾". Cut the square in half diagonally twice to make 4 triangles (C).

- Make 4 triangles using template D. Flip the template and make 4 D reverse. Draw single and double hash marks on the seam allowances as noted on the template.

3. From green fabric:

- Cut 2 squares 1⅞" × 1⅞". Cut each square in half diagonally once to make 4 triangles (A).

- Cut 1 square 2" × 2" (E).

- Make 4 triangles using template F. Draw single hash marks on the seam allowances as noted on the template.

4. Sew 3 light beige A triangles to each green A triangle to make 4 block corners as shown in the block assembly diagram. Press.

5. Matching hash marks for correct placement, sew a light brown D and a light brown D reverse to each green F triangle. Press.

6. Sew 2 light brown C triangles to opposite sides of the green E square. Press. Sew the remaining light brown C triangles to the other 2 sides to make the block center. Press.

7. Sewing from point to point only, sew 2 D/F/D reverse units to opposite sides of the block center.

8. Sewing from point to point only and using the hash marks to indicate the appropriate sides, sew 2 light beige B triangles to opposite sides of the remaining D/F/D reverse units.

9. Use Y-seam construction to sew the units created in Step 8 to the block center, following the direction and order indicated in the block assembly diagram. Press.

10. Sew on the 4 block corners. Press.

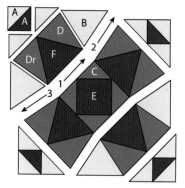

The template pattern is on page 122.

1. From light beige fabric:

- Cut 8 squares 2⅛″ × 2⅛″ (A).

- Cut 2 A squares in half diagonally once to make 4 triangles (B).

- Make 4 trapezoids using template C. Flip the template and make 4 C reverses.

- Cut 1 square 2¾″ × 2¾″ (D).

2. From red fabric, cut 1 square 3½″ × 3½″. Cut the square in half twice diagonally to make 4 triangles (E).

3. From medium blue fabric, cut 6 squares 2⅛″ × 2⅛″ (A).

4. Sew 2 red E triangles to opposite sides of the light beige D square. Press. Sew the remaining red E triangles to the other 2 sides to make the block center. Press.

5. Refer to Quick-Pieced HST Units (page 14, Abel's Favorite, Step 3) to make 12 quick-pieced HST units with the 6 medium blue A squares and 6 of the light beige A squares.

Following the block assembly diagram for correct placement, complete the following steps:

6. Sew 2 HST units together. Press. Repeat to make a second pair. Sew 2 HST units together to make a mirror-image pair. Press. Repeat to make a second mirror-image pair.

7. Sew a light beige B triangle to the remaining 4 HST units. Press.

8. Sew each unit created in Step 6 to a unit created in Step 7, referring to the block assembly diagram for placement. Press.

9. Sew a light beige C and a light beige C reverse to each unit created in Step 8 to make 4 block corners. Press.

10. Sewing from point to point only, sew 2 block corners to opposite sides of the block center. Use Y-seam construction, following the order and direction indicated in the block assembly diagram, to sew the remaining block corners to the other 2 sides. Press.

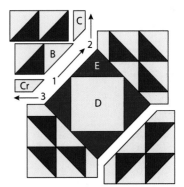

1. From light beige fabric:

- Cut 6 squares 2⅜″ × 2⅜″ (A).

- Cut 4 squares 2″ × 2″ (B).

2. From dark brown fabric, cut 3 squares 2⅜″ × 2⅜″ (A).

3. From red fabric, cut 3 squares 2⅜″ × 2⅜″ (A).

4. Refer to Quick-Pieced HST Units (page 14, Abel's Favorite, Step 3) to make 6 quick-pieced HST units with the 3 red A squares and 3 of the light beige A squares.

5. Repeat Step 4 with the remaining light beige A squares and the dark brown A squares to make 6 light beige and dark brown HST units.

Following the block assembly diagram for correct placement, complete the following steps:

6. Sew 2 dark brown / light beige HST units together as shown in the block assembly diagram. Press. Repeat to make a second pair. Make 2 red / light beige mirror-image pairs.

7. Sew a light beige B square to each remaining dark brown / light beige triangle-square and each red / light beige triangle-square. Press.

8. Sew each dark brown unit from Step 6 to a dark brown unit from Step 7 to make 2 block quarters. Press. Sew each red unit from Step 6 to a red unit from Step 7 to make 2 block quarters. Press.

9. Sew the block quarters into 2 rows as shown. Press. Sew the rows together. Press.

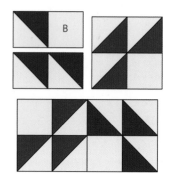

The template pattern is on page 122.

1. From light beige fabric:

- Cut 2 squares 2½″ × 2½″. Cut each square in half diagonally twice to make 8 triangles (D).

- Cut 4 squares 1⅜″ × 1⅜″ (E).

- Cut 4 squares 1¾″ × 1¾″. Cut each square in half diagonally once to make 8 triangles (F).

2. From red fabric:

- Cut 1 square 4¼″ × 4¼″. Cut the square in half diagonally twice to make 4 triangles (B).

- Make 8 rhombuses using template C.

3. From green fabric:

- Cut 1 square 3½″ × 3½″ (A).

- Make 8 rhombuses using template C.

Following the block assembly diagram for correct placement, complete the following steps:

4. Sewing from point to point only and not into the seam allowances, sew each red C rhombus to a green C rhombus. Press. Make 4 pairs and 4 mirror-image pairs.

5. Use Y-seam construction to sew a light beige D triangle to each pair created in Step 4. Press

6. Sewing only from point to point, sew 1 light beige E square to each of 4 identical C/C/D units. Press. Sew each of these units to a mirror-image C/C/D unit. Press. Sew 2 light beige F triangles to opposite sides of each unit. Press. Repeat to make 4 block corners.

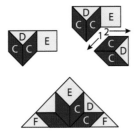

7. Sew 2 red B triangles to opposite sides of the green A square. Press. Sew the remaining red B triangles to the other 2 sides to make the block center. Press

8. Sew 2 block corners to opposite sides of the block center. Press. Sew the remaining block corners to the other sides of the block center. Press.

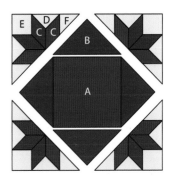

General Instructions

SASHING AND BORDERS

Cutting

Yardage is calculated assuming a 42" usable width of fabric.

Fine stripe or dark brown:
- Cut 8 strips 6½" × width of fabric. Cut into 220 short sashing strips 1½" × 6½".

Light brown:
- Cut 4 strips 1½" × 84" on the lengthwise grain of the fabric for the inner border.
  Option: Cut 9 strips 1½" × width of fabric. Sew diagonally end to end. Subcut into 4 inner border strips 1½" × 84".

- Cut 5 strips 1½" × remaining width of fabric *(cut 4 strips if cutting from full width of fabric)*. Cut into 100 cornerstone squares 1½" × 1½".

Wide stripe:
- Cut 4 strips 10½" × 103" on the lengthwise grain of the fabric for the outer border.
  Note: The width of your outer border will vary according to the width of the stripe in your fabric. Cut to the most attractive width, remembering to add a ¼" seam allowance to both long edges.

QUILT ASSEMBLY

1. Arrange the sampler blocks in 11 rows of 11 blocks. Sew the blocks together with 110 of the short sashing strips (10 per row). Press the seams toward the sashing strips.

2. Sew 11 short sashing strips together, separated by the light brown cornerstones. Press toward the sashing strips. Repeat to make a total of 10 sashing rows.

3. Sew the sampler block rows together, separated by the sashing rows. Press toward the sashing rows.

4. Sew each light brown inner border, centered along the length, to a wide stripe outer border. Press toward the outer border.

5. Refer to your favorite basic quilting book to add mitered borders to the quilt. Press toward the borders.

6. Refer to your favorite basic quilting book to layer the quilt top, batting, and backing. Baste. Quilt as desired. Attach a hanging sleeve and bind.

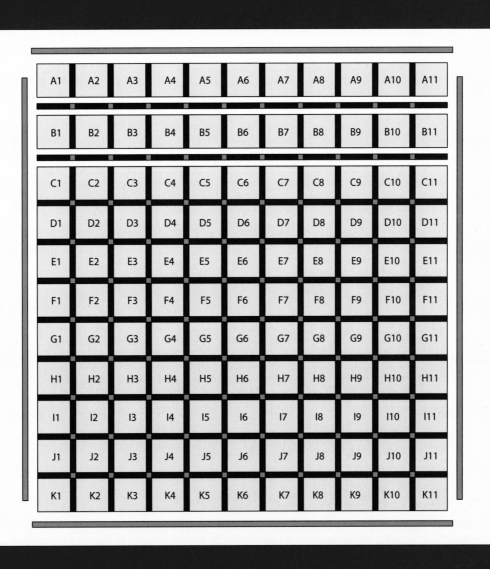

Quilt assembly diagram

The Gallery

RHAPSODY IN BLUE, 92″ × 92″,
designed and assembled by Jennifer Chiaverini, pieced by Jennifer
Chiaverini and friends, machine quilted by Sue Vollbrecht, 2012.

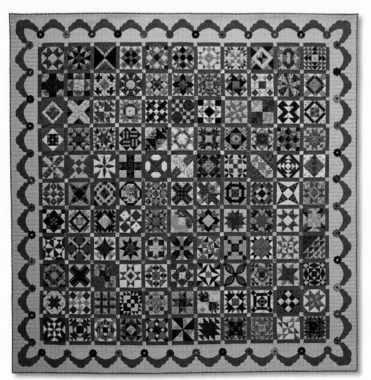

THE PURPLE STORY, 94″ × 94″,
hand pieced and hand quilted by Annelies van den Bergh, 2012.

MERRY MERRY JANUARY, 64″ × 80″,
designed and assembled by Jennifer Chiaverini, pieced by Jennifer Chiaverini and friends,
machine quilted by Sue Vollbrecht, 2012. The "Elm Creek Quilts: New Year's Quilt Collection"
fabrics used in this quilt were provided by Red Rooster Fabrics.

ELIZABETH THE SECOND, 62″ × 78″,
designed and assembled by Jennifer Chiaverini, pieced by Jennifer Chiaverini and friends, machine quilted by Sue Vollbrecht, 2012. The "Elm Creek Quilts: Elizabeth's Collection" fabrics used in this quilt were provided by Red Rooster Fabrics.

ELIZABETH THE FIRST, 76½″ × 76½″,
designed and assembled by Jennifer Chiaverini, pieced by
Jennifer Chiaverini and friends, machine quilted by Sue
Vollbrecht, 2012. The "Elm Creek Quilts: Elizabeth's
Collection" fabrics used in this quilt were provided by
Red Rooster Fabrics.

AUTUMNAL TINTS, 100″ × 100″,
designed and assembled by Jennifer Chiaverini, pieced by
Jennifer Chiaverini and friends, machine quilted by Sue
Vollbrecht, 2012. The "Elm Creek Quilts: Cross Country
Quilters Collection" fabrics used in this quilt were provided
by Red Rooster Fabrics.

SANTA ROSA SUNSET, 49″ × 49″,
designed by Jennifer Chiaverini, pieced by Jennifer Chiaverini and friends,
quilted by Sue Vollbrecht, 2012. The "Elm Creek Quilts: Rosa's Collection"
fabrics used in this quilt were provided by Red Rooster Fabrics.

ANNE IDA'S LOYAL UNION SAMPLER, 90″ × 90″,
pieced and machine quilted by Anne Ida Røkeness, 2012.

AULANI HO'OILO, 62″ × 80″,
designed and assembled by Jennifer Chiaverini, pieced
by Jennifer Chiaverini and friends, machine quilted
by Sue Vollbrecht, 2012. The "Elm Creek Quilts: The
Aloha Quilt Collection" fabrics used in this quilt were
provided by Red Rooster Fabrics.

Template and Foundation Patterns

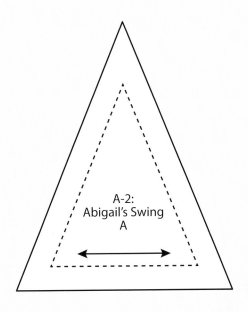

A-2:
Abigail's Swing
A

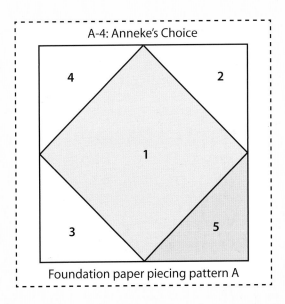

A-4: Anneke's Choice

4

2

1

3

5

Foundation paper piecing pattern A

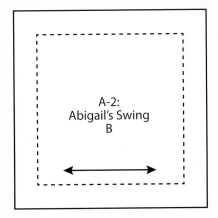

A-2:
Abigail's Swing
B

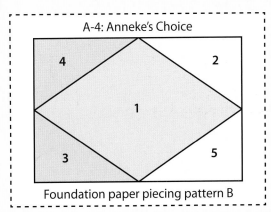

A-4: Anneke's Choice

4

2

1

3

5

Foundation paper piecing pattern B

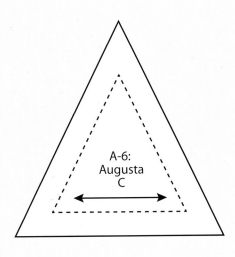

A-6:
Augusta
C

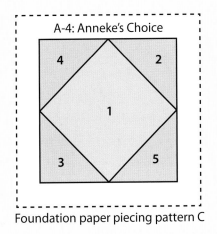

A-4: Anneke's Choice

4

2

1

3

5

Foundation paper piecing pattern C

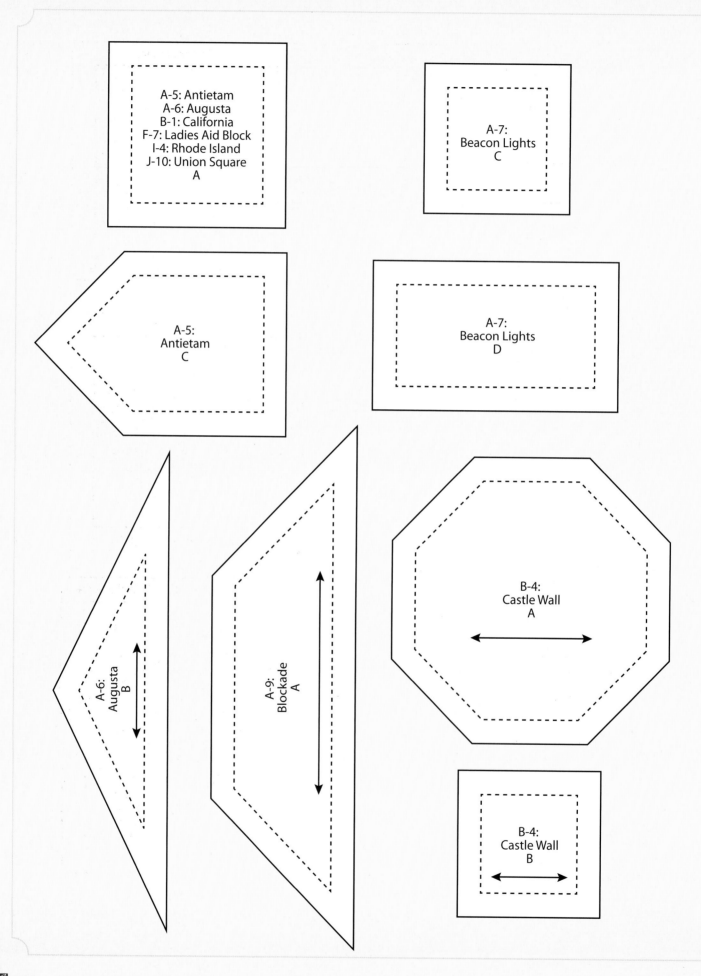

A-5: Antietam
A-6: Augusta
B-1: California
F-7: Ladies Aid Block
I-4: Rhode Island
J-10: Union Square
A

A-7:
Beacon Lights
C

A-5:
Antietam
C

A-7:
Beacon Lights
D

A-6:
Augusta
B

A-9:
Blockade
A

B-4:
Castle Wall
A

B-4:
Castle Wall
B

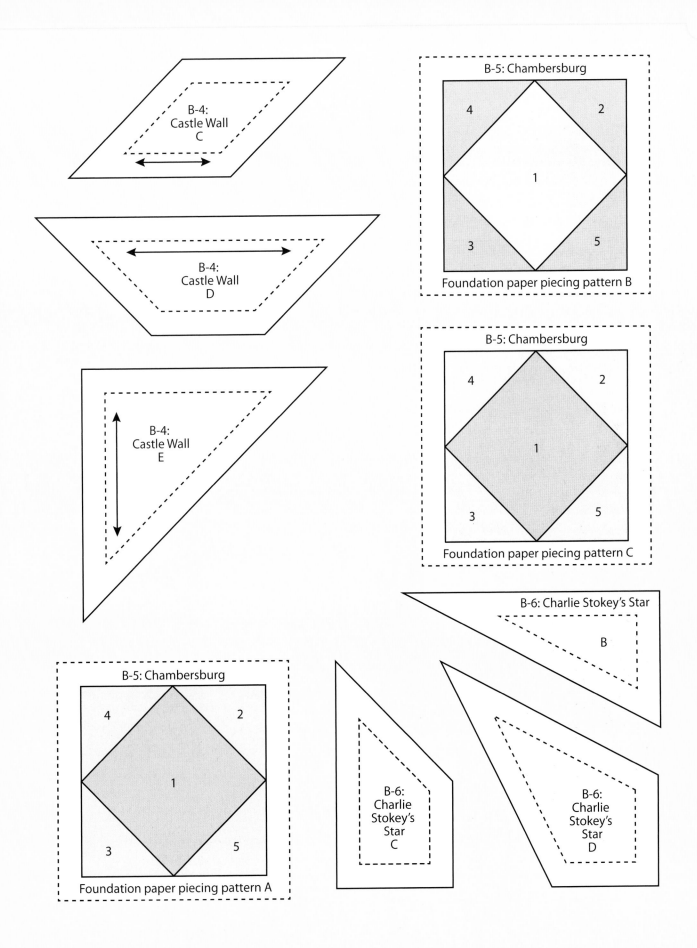

B-4:
Castle Wall
C

B-4:
Castle Wall
D

B-4:
Castle Wall
E

B-5: Chambersburg

4

2

1

3

5

Foundation paper piecing pattern B

B-5: Chambersburg

4

2

1

3

5

Foundation paper piecing pattern C

B-6: Charlie Stokey's Star

B

B-6:
Charlie
Stokey's
Star
C

B-6:
Charlie
Stokey's
Star
D

B-5: Chambersburg

4

2

1

3

5

Foundation paper piecing pattern A

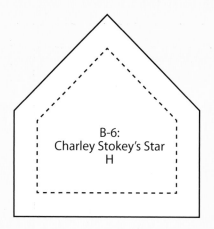

B-6:
Charley Stokey's Star
H

B-7:
Christmas
Star
D

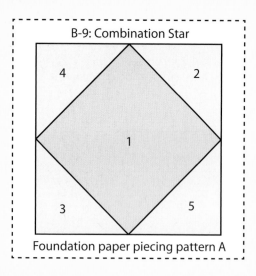

B-9: Combination Star

4   2

1

3   5

Foundation paper piecing pattern A

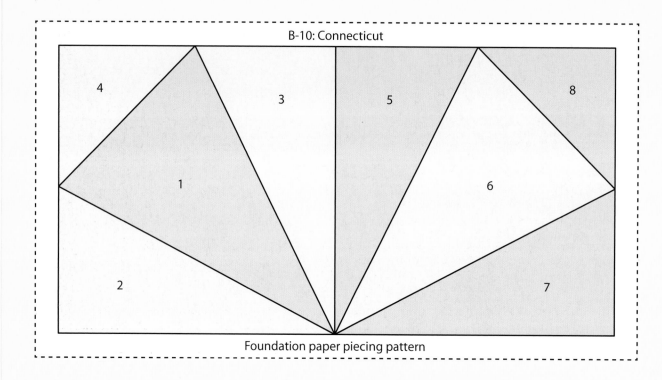

B-10: Connecticut

4   3   5   8

1   6

2   7

Foundation paper piecing pattern

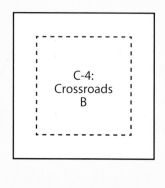

C-4:
Crossroads
B

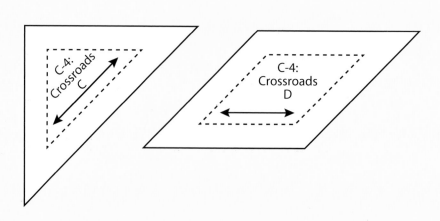

C-4:
Crossroads
C

C-4:
Crossroads
D

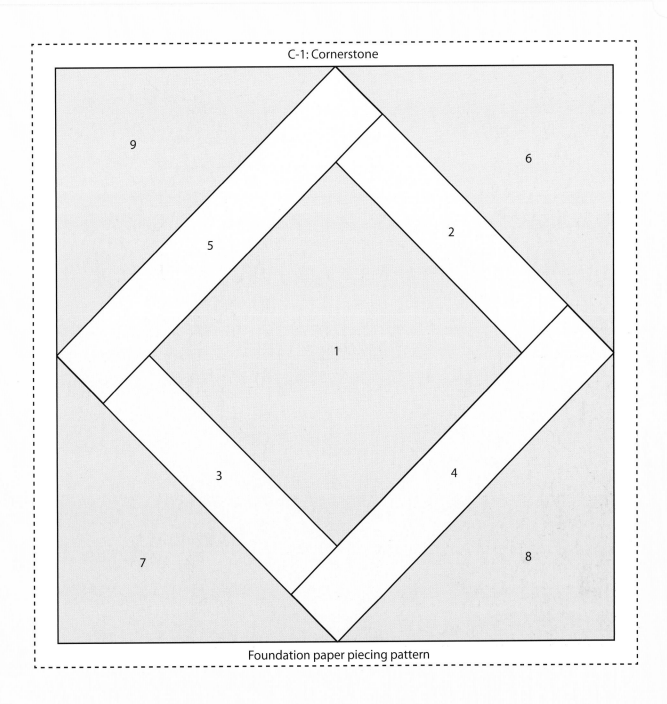

C-1: Cornerstone

9

6

2

5

1

3

4

7

8

Foundation paper piecing pattern

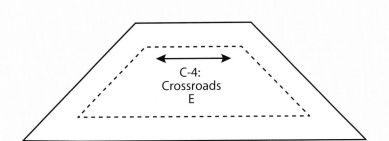

C-4:
Crossroads
E

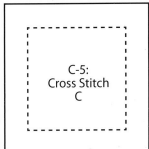

C-5:
Cross Stitch
C

C-5:
Cross Stitch
D

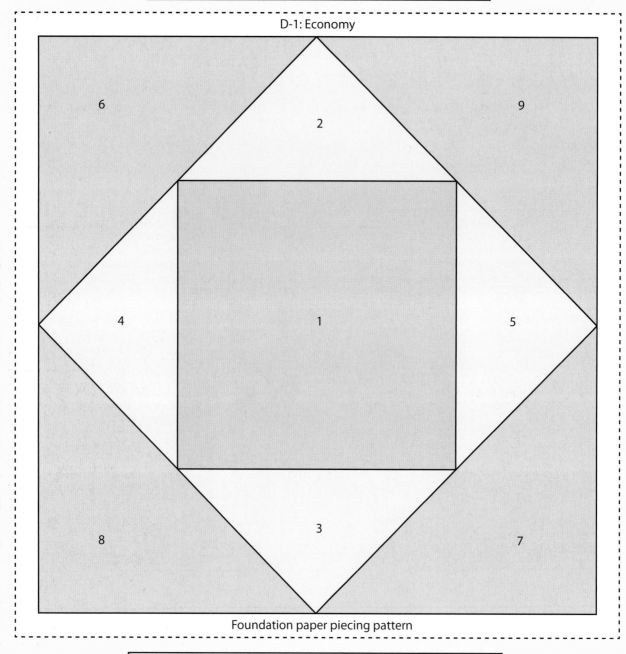

D-1: Economy

6

9

2

4

1

5

8

3

7

Foundation paper piecing pattern

C-11:
Drummer Boy
E

The Loyal Union Sampler from Elm Creek Quilts

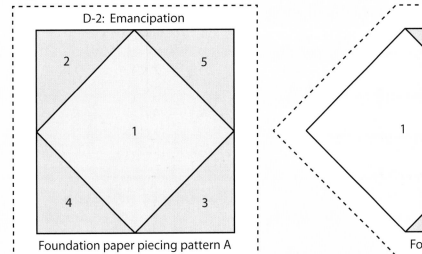

D-2: Emancipation

2 5

1

4 3

Foundation paper piecing pattern A

D-2: Emancipation

2 5

1 4

3 6

Foundation paper piecing pattern B

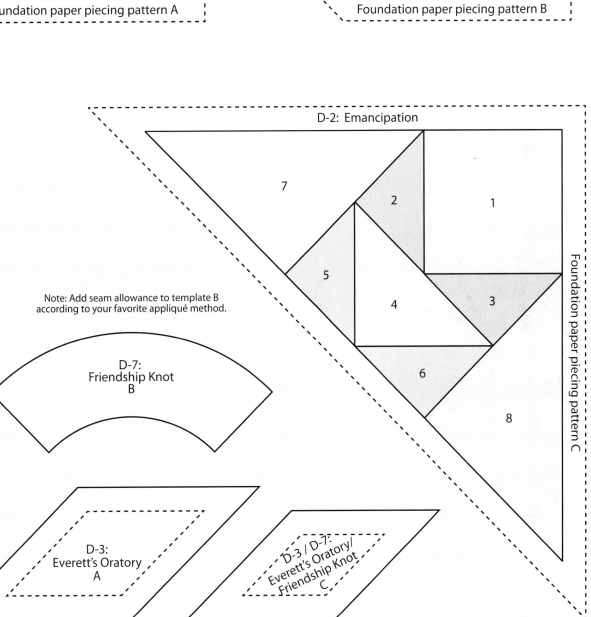

D-2: Emancipation

7

2

1

5

4

3

6

8

Foundation paper piecing pattern C

Note: Add seam allowance to template B according to your favorite appliqué method.

D-7: Friendship Knot B

D-3: Everett's Oratory A

D-3 / D-7: Everett's Oratory/ Friendship Knot C

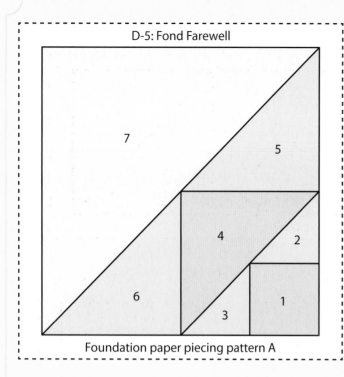

D-5: Fond Farewell

Foundation paper piecing pattern A

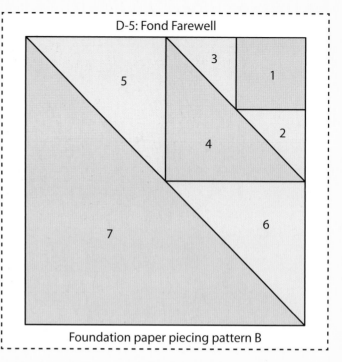

D-5: Fond Farewell

Foundation paper piecing pattern B

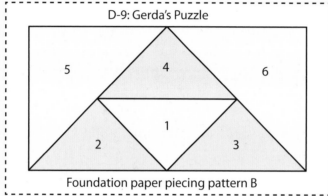

D-9: Gerda's Puzzle

Foundation paper piecing pattern B

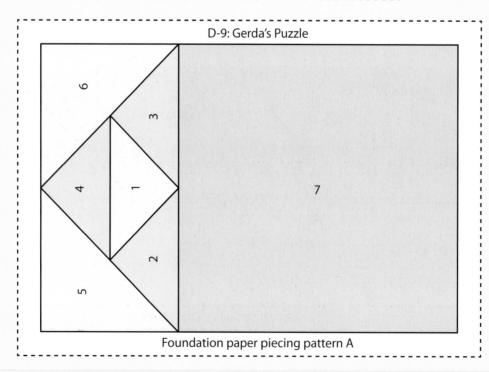

D-9: Gerda's Puzzle

Foundation paper piecing pattern A

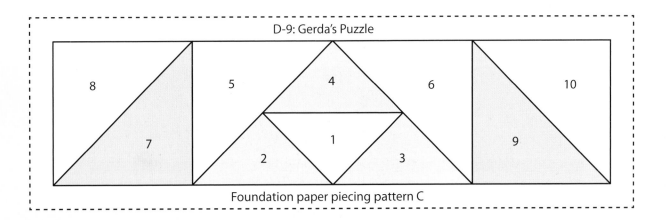

D-9: Gerda's Puzzle

Foundation paper piecing pattern C

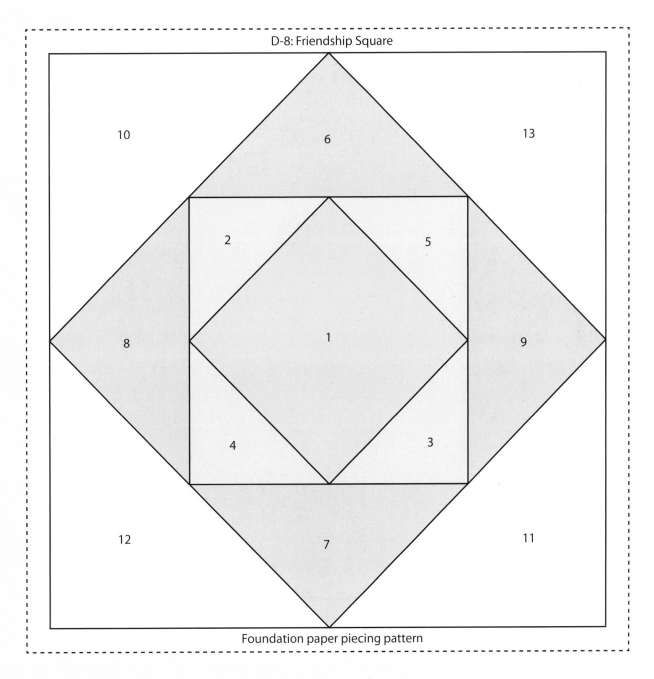

D-8: Friendship Square

Foundation paper piecing pattern

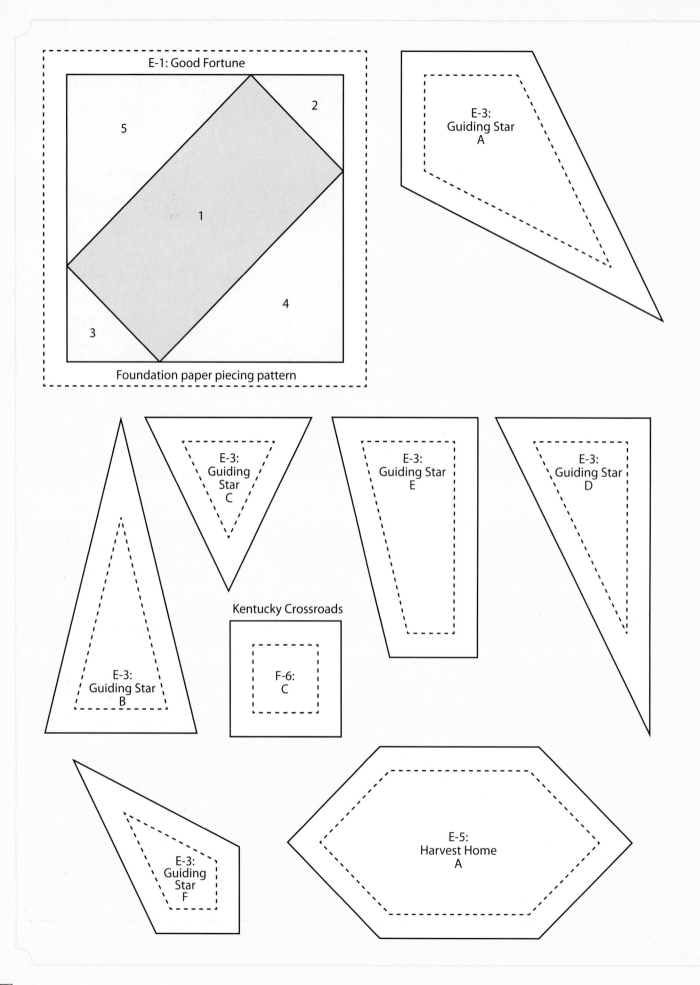

E-1: Good Fortune

5

2

1

3

4

Foundation paper piecing pattern

E-3:
Guiding Star
A

E-3:
Guiding
Star
C

E-3:
Guiding Star
E

E-3:
Guiding Star
D

E-3:
Guiding Star
B

Kentucky Crossroads

F-6:
C

E-3:
Guiding
Star
F

E-5:
Harvest Home
A

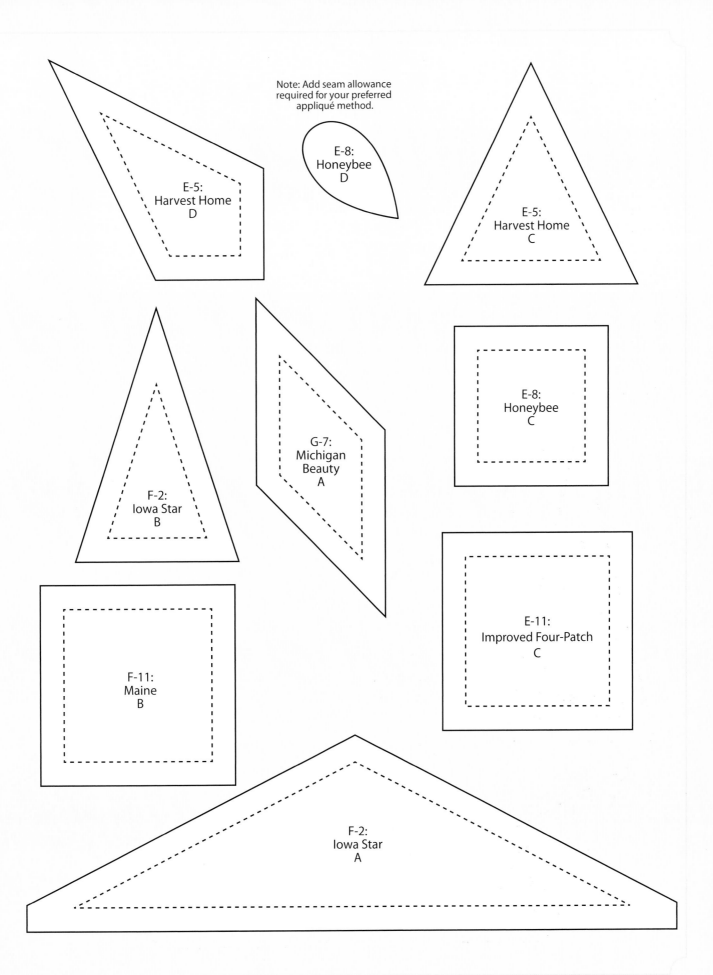

Note: Add seam allowance required for your preferred appliqué method.

E-5:
Harvest Home
D

E-8:
Honeybee
D

E-5:
Harvest Home
C

G-7:
Michigan
Beauty
A

E-8:
Honeybee
C

F-2:
Iowa Star
B

E-11:
Improved Four-Patch
C

F-11:
Maine
B

F-2:
Iowa Star
A

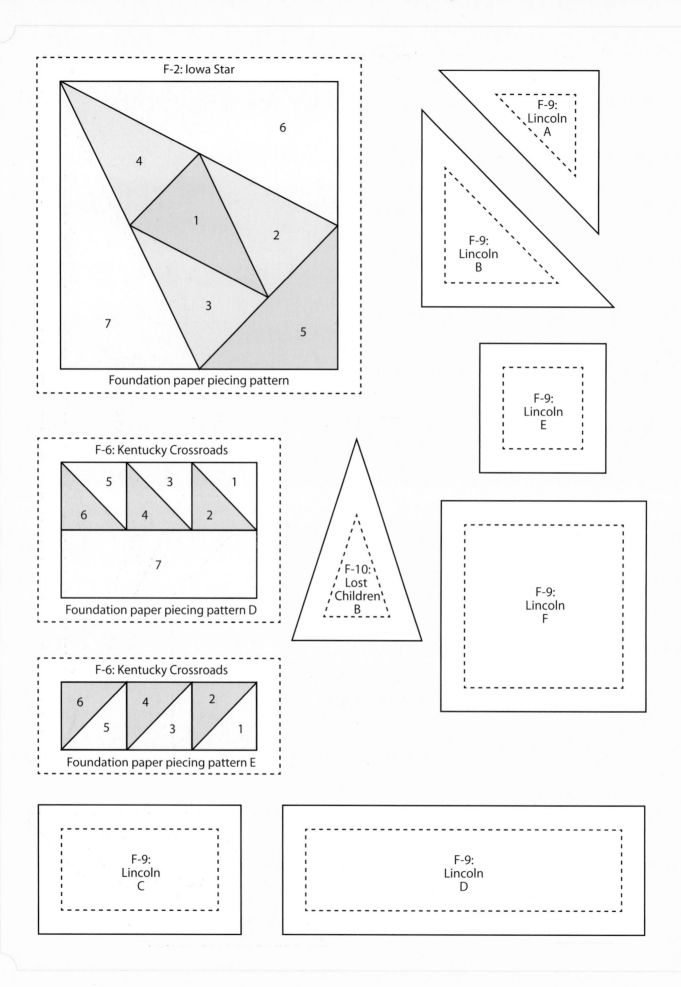

F-2: Iowa Star

4
6
1
2
3
7
5

Foundation paper piecing pattern

F-6: Kentucky Crossroads

5 3 1
6 4 2
7

Foundation paper piecing pattern D

F-6: Kentucky Crossroads

6 4 2
5 3 1

Foundation paper piecing pattern E

F-9: Lincoln A

F-9: Lincoln B

F-9: Lincoln E

F-10: Lost Children B

F-9: Lincoln F

F-9: Lincoln C

F-9: Lincoln D

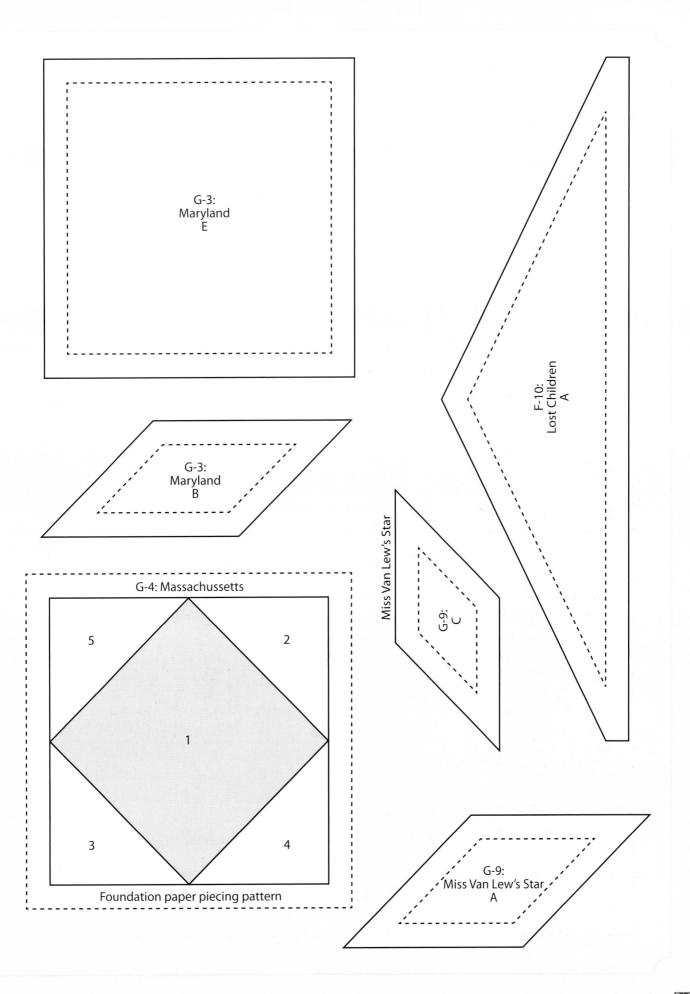

G-3:
Maryland
E

G-3:
Maryland
B

F-10:
Lost Children
A

Miss Van Lew's Star

G-9:
C

G-4: Massachussetts

5

2

1

3

4

Foundation paper piecing pattern

G-9:
Miss Van Lew's Star
A

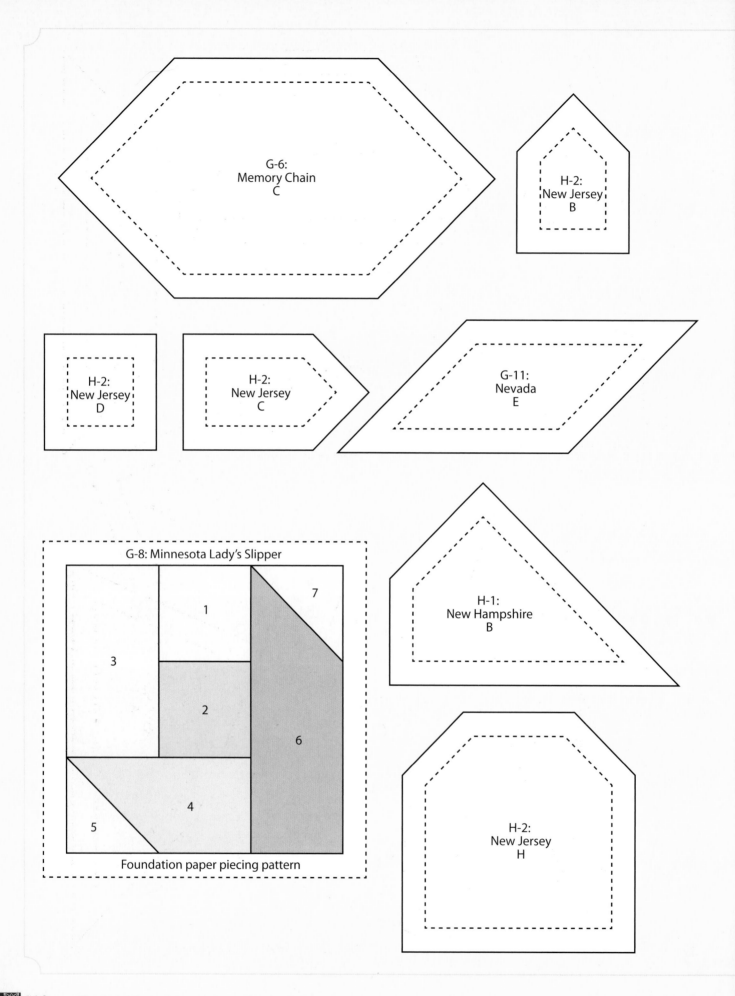

G-6:
Memory Chain
C

H-2:
New Jersey
B

H-2:
New Jersey
D

H-2:
New Jersey
C

G-11:
Nevada
E

G-8: Minnesota Lady's Slipper

1

3

2

7

6

4

5

Foundation paper piecing pattern

H-1:
New Hampshire
B

H-2:
New Jersey
H

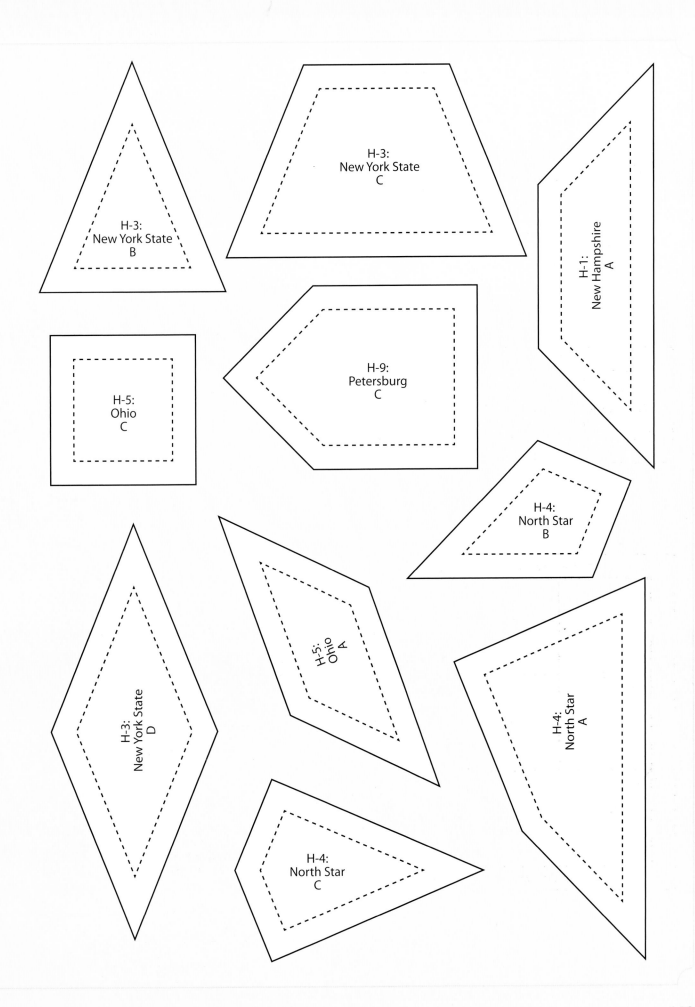

H-3:
New York State
B

H-3:
New York State
C

H-1:
New Hampshire
A

H-5:
Ohio
C

H-9:
Petersburg
C

H-4:
North Star
B

H-3:
New York State
D

H-5:
Ohio
A

H-4:
North Star
A

H-4:
North Star
C

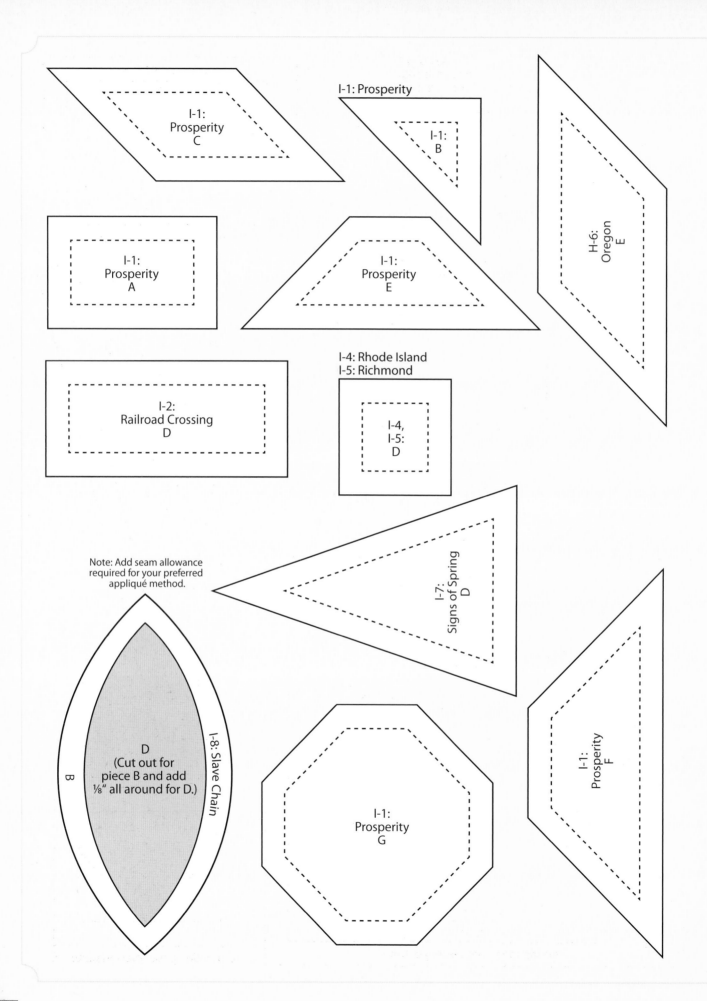

I-1: Prosperity
C

I-1: Prosperity

I-1:
B

H-6:
Oregon
E

I-1:
Prosperity
A

I-1:
Prosperity
E

I-2:
Railroad Crossing
D

I-4: Rhode Island
I-5: Richmond

I-4,
I-5:
D

I-7:
Signs of Spring
D

Note: Add seam allowance required for your preferred appliqué method.

D
(Cut out for piece B and add ⅛" all around for D.)

B

I-8: Slave Chain

I-1:
Prosperity
F

I-1:
Prosperity
G

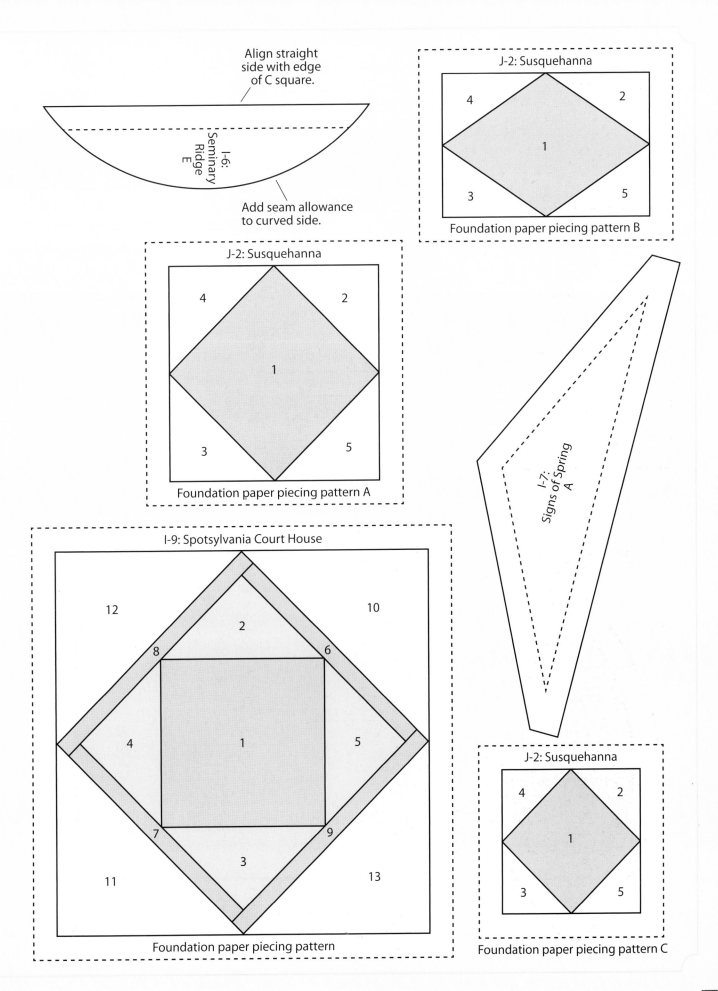

Align straight side with edge of C square.

I-6:
Seminary
Ridge
E

Add seam allowance to curved side.

J-2: Susquehanna

4 2

1

3 5

Foundation paper piecing pattern B

J-2: Susquehanna

4 2

1

3 5

Foundation paper piecing pattern A

I-7:
Signs of Spring
A

I-9: Spotsylvania Court House

12   10

2

8   6

4   1   5

7   9

3

11   13

Foundation paper piecing pattern

J-2: Susquehanna

4 2

1

3 5

Foundation paper piecing pattern C

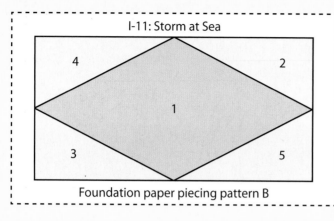

I-11: Storm at Sea

Foundation paper piecing pattern B

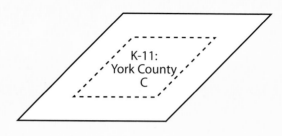

K-11:
York County
C

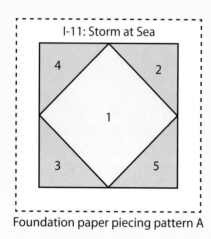

I-11: Storm at Sea

Foundation paper piecing pattern A

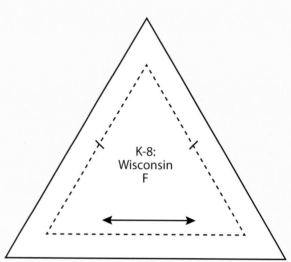

K-8:
Wisconsin
F

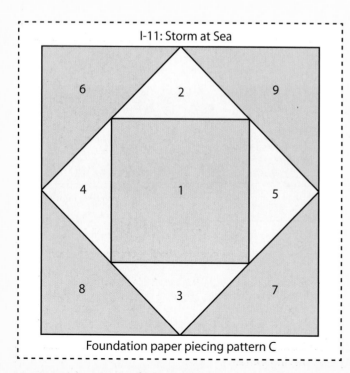

I-11: Storm at Sea

Foundation paper piecing pattern C

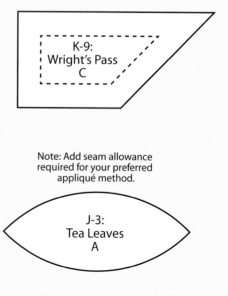

K-9:
Wright's Pass
C

Note: Add seam allowance
required for your preferred
appliqué method.

J-3:
Tea Leaves
A

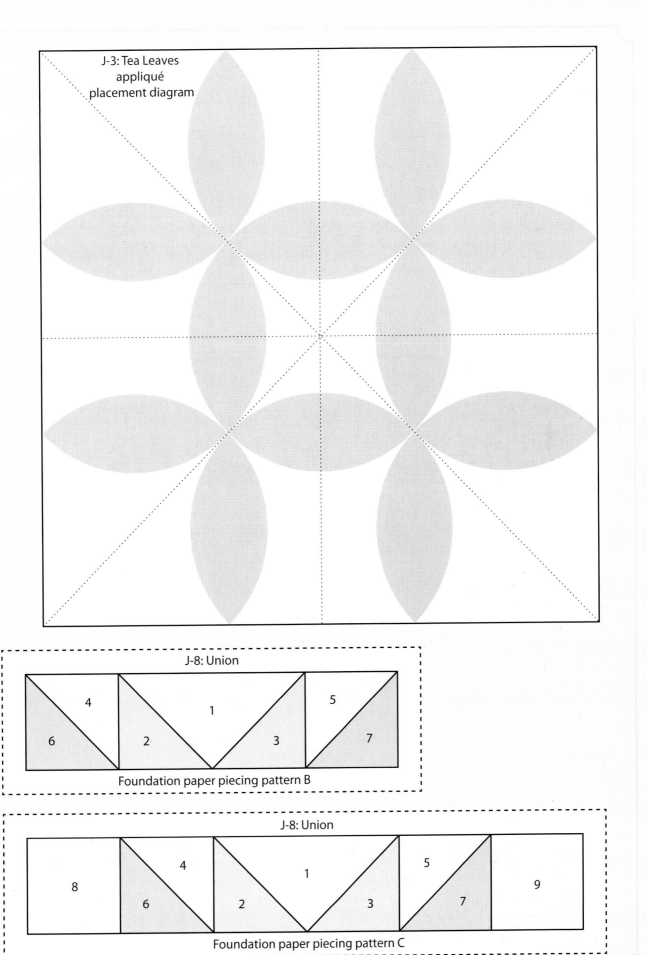

J-3: Tea Leaves
appliqué
placement diagram

J-8: Union

Foundation paper piecing pattern B

J-8: Union

Foundation paper piecing pattern C

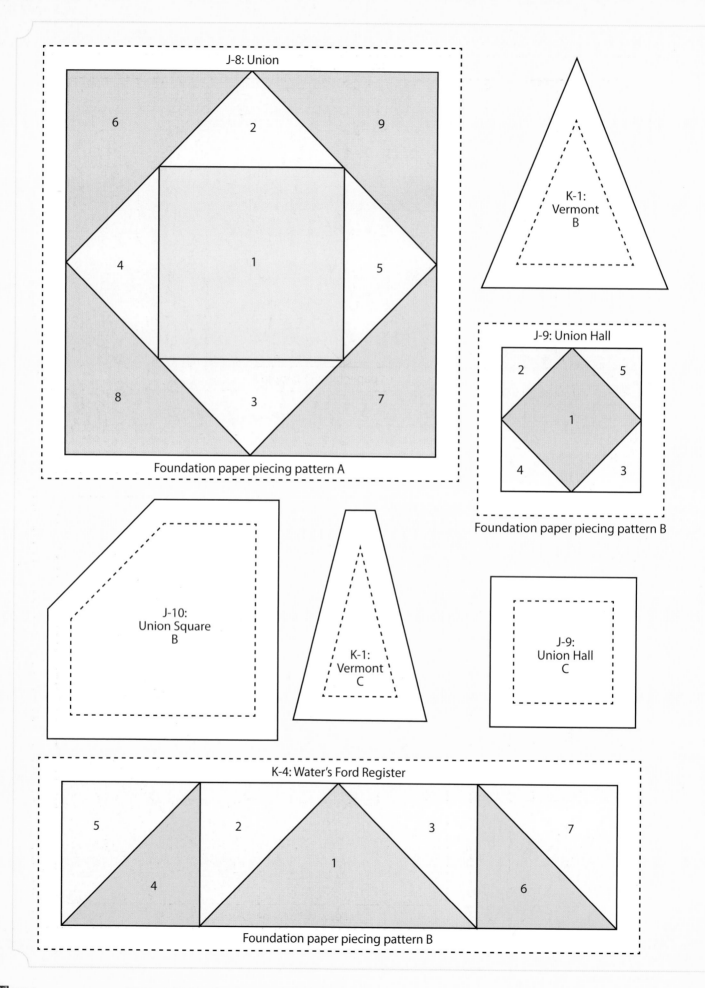

J-8: Union

6   2   9

4   1   5

8   3   7

Foundation paper piecing pattern A

K-1:
Vermont
B

J-9: Union Hall

2   5
1
4   3

Foundation paper piecing pattern B

J-10:
Union Square
B

K-1:
Vermont
C

J-9:
Union Hall
C

K-4: Water's Ford Register

5   2   3   7
4   1   6

Foundation paper piecing pattern B

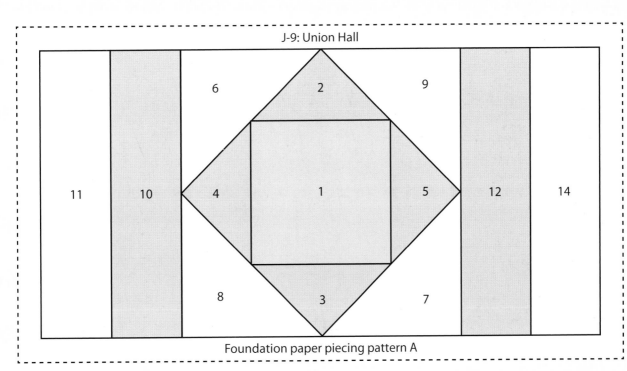

J-9: Union Hall

Foundation paper piecing pattern A

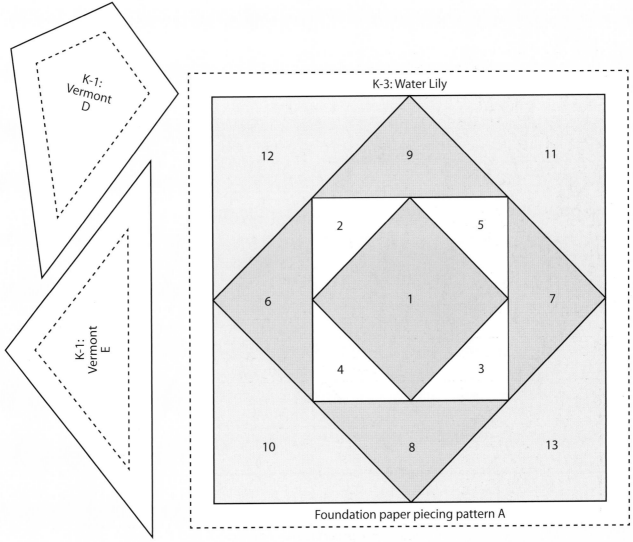

K-1: Vermont D

K-1: Vermont E

K-3: Water Lily

Foundation paper piecing pattern A

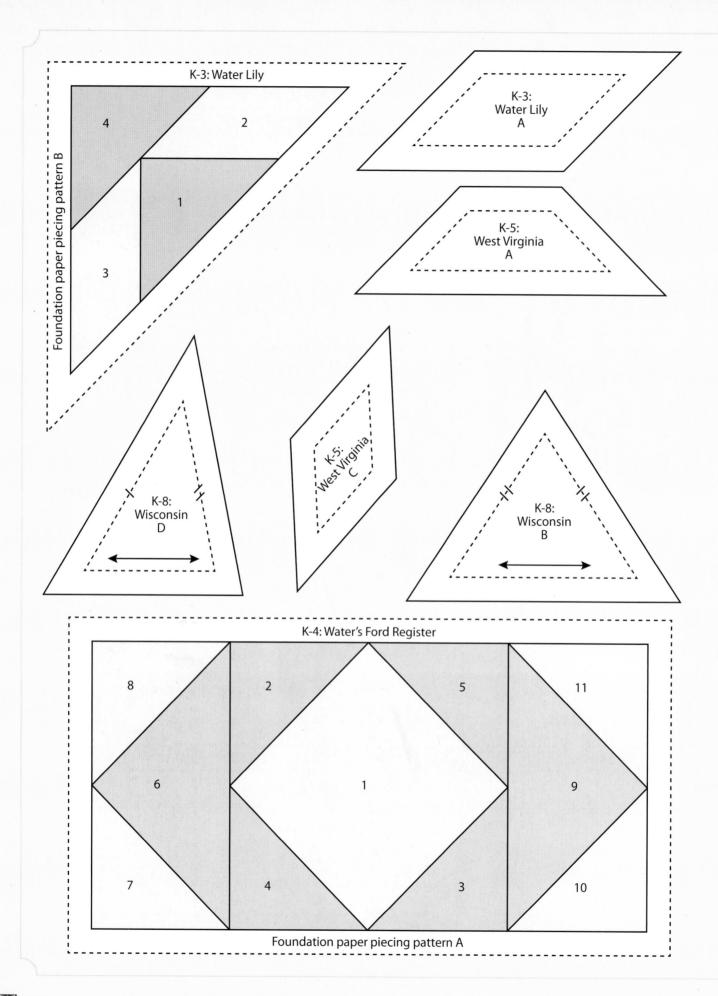

K-3: Water Lily

Foundation paper piecing pattern B

4

2

1

3

K-3:
Water Lily
A

K-5:
West Virginia
A

K-8:
Wisconsin
D

K-5:
West Virginia
C

K-8:
Wisconsin
B

K-4: Water's Ford Register

8

2

5

11

6

1

9

7

4

3

10

Foundation paper piecing pattern A

The Loyal Union Sampler from Elm Creek Quilts

About the Author

Jennifer Chiaverini is the author of the *New York Times* best-selling Elm Creek Quilts series, as well as five previous collections of quilt patterns from C&T Publishing inspired by her novels. Her most recent novels are *Mrs. Lincoln's Dressmaker* and *The Spymistress*. Her original quilt designs have been featured in *Country Woman*, *Quiltmaker*, and *Quilt*, and her short stories have appeared in *Quiltmaker* and *Quilters Newsletter*. A graduate of the University of Notre Dame and the University of Chicago, she lives with her husband and two sons in Madison, Wisconsin.

Also by Jennifer Chiaverini:

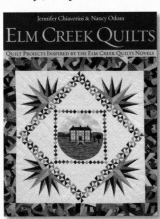

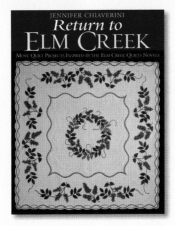

Great Titles *from* C&T PUBLISHING

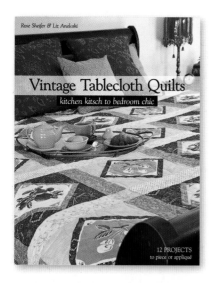

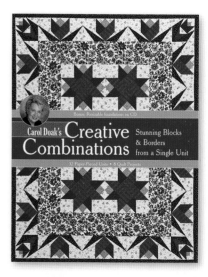

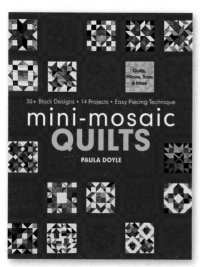

Available at your local retailer or **www.ctpub.com** *or* **800-284-1114**

For a list of other fine books from C&T Publishing, visit our website to view our catalog online.

C&T PUBLISHING, INC.

P.O. Box 1456
Lafayette, CA 94549
800-284-1114

Email: ctinfo@ctpub.com
Website: www.ctpub.com

C&T Publishing's professional photography services are now available to the public. Visit us at www.ctmediaservices.com.

Tips and Techniques can be found at www.ctpub.com > Consumer Resources > Quiltmaking Basics: Tips & Techniques for Quiltmaking & More

For quilting supplies:

COTTON PATCH

1025 Brown Ave.
Lafayette, CA 94549

Store: 925-284-1177
Mail order: 925-283-7883

Email: CottonPa@aol.com
Website: www.quiltusa.com

Note: Fabrics shown may not be currently available, as fabric manufacturers keep most fabrics in print for only a short time.